PS
758
.B6
.

Bowde
Wea

Philip Freneau

DATE			

Twayne's United States Authors Series

Sylvia E. Bowman, *Editor*

INDIANA UNIVERSITY

Philip Freneau

TUSAS 260

J. Halpin

PHILIP FRENEAU

By MARY WEATHERSPOON BOWDEN

University of Texas at Austin"

TWAYNE PUBLISHERS

A DIVISION OF G. K. HALL & CO., BOSTON

Copyright © 1976 by G. K. Hall & Co.
All Rights Reserved
First Printing

Library of Congress Cataloging in Publication Data

Bowden, Mary Weatherspoon.
  Philip Freneau.

  (Twayne's United States authors series; TUSAS 260)
  Bibliography: p. 181–85.
  Includes index.
  1. Freneau, Philip Morin, 1752–1832.
PS758.B6   811'.2   [B]   75–30651
ISBN 0–8057–7161–1

To my family

Contents

About the Author

The author, Mary Weatherspoon Bowden, was born and raised in Johnston, Iowa and received her bachelor's degree from the University of Nebraska. She held a teaching assistantship at the University of Texas where she completed her master's degree and Ph.D. During this time she developed her interest in the influence of politics on literature, an interest which has led to this book.

The author was an assistant professor at Indiana University at Fort Wayne, and has taught at the University of Texas. Her research interests include Philip Freneau, Washington Irving, and Cotton Mather. In addition to her doctoral dissertation on the relation of political beliefs to literature in the work of Freneau and Irving, Professor Bowden has written and published on Irving.

Preface

In the period between the Revolutionary War and the War of 1812, Philip Morin Freneau is one of the most important literary figures. He holds this position not just because he was a prolific writer but because he experimented with many different styles and forms. In the body of his works one can find poems which illustrate well the neoclassic school and those which classically illustrate the pre-Romantic fancy. He is, therefore, important as a transitional poet. His poems about the sea, the Indian, and the mutability of life are intrinsically good—as are his poems mocking these genres. His occasional poems are justly celebrated for their satire and realism, and they illustrate that genre well. In considering his value as a litterateur, we must also remember Freneau's prose; for he tried his hand at the philosophic essay as well as the satiric diatribe.

But a study of Freneau should go beyond evaluating his works. Freneau is important precisely because he is, in many ways, a man representative of his time; and the time he lived in is historically important. Freneau shared the same kind of basic education as his more famous contemporaries, Thomas Jefferson and James Madison. Like many others, he studied theology and became disillusioned with it. He, like others, fled the Revolutionary War, but he also became an enthusiastic believer in its cause. He put aside poetry to propagandize and then returned to poetry. He made the sea his career at a time when the sea was a major employer. He became a political-party worker and a newspaper editor for the party. He joined in the Americans' initial enthusiasm for the French Revolution; he admired Thomas Paine. His attention was caught not only by the national and international events, but also by state and local causes. And always, he wrote poetry.

Freneau reflects the Enlightenment most strongly in the variety of his interests: in deism, in anthropology, in the origin of the Indians, in balloon ascensions, in how to categorize plants. His mind was open to all current influences and events—in theology, philosophy, aesthetics, science, government—the list goes on and on. But Freneau did not stop with consideration of the ideas or the events; he put them into prose or verse form. He was respected as a scholar and a gentleman of learning; but, at the same time, he represented the other side of the age, the side that produced the excesses of the French Revolution and, from Freneau, vituperative editorials. And all the while he looked for the day when poetry would be appreciated by his countrymen, but lack of appreciation never stopped him from writing. In his poetry and prose we see reflected, therefore, the interests and events of the age he lived in—an age in which his diversity was most natural.

Freneau's greatest claim to attention is the variety shown in his works—a variety which reflects his many interests. Thus, perhaps more than most authors, it is difficult to separate Freneau and his times. There are four outstanding occurrences in Freneau's life—his college years, the Revolutionary War, his editorships of the 1790s, and his successful 1809 edition of poetry; and these events are used as the basis for my organization. Chapter 1 deals with the training given to Freneau in college and with his first works, which show the variety which always marked him. Chapter 2 covers his verse on current events, the most famous being, of course, his war poems. Chapter 3 deals with his newspaper editing and his prose essays which appeared in the newspapers. And Chapter 4 treats his nonoccasional verse, poetry not inspired by any particular event, but poems which, in his later years, he smoothed and polished. Although, except for the first chapter, each chapter deals with one genre and the time-span in which Freneau concentrated on that genre, we should remember that at no time did he limit himself to one genre, one style, one tone, one interest. Because Freneau was interested in all things, he never concentrated on one: he produced few masterpieces, but his work as a whole is fascinating in its scope.

In quoting the poetry, I have followed the text of F. L. Pattee's *Poems of Philip Freneau* or Lewis Leary's *The Last Poems of Philip Freneau*. For poems not included in these volumes, I have used the original editions of Freneau's lifetime. For the prose, I have gone to its first printing in the newspapers, except, where noted, I have used Philip Marsh's *The Prose of Philip Freneau*. Lewis Leary's *That Rascal Freneau* has been valuable as a guide.

Special thanks go to my husband Edwin; to my parents, James and Margaret Weatherspoon, and to my family.

MARY WEATHERSPOON BOWDEN

Chronology

1752   Philip Morin Freneau born January 2 (Old Style).

1768   Entered College of New Jersey.

1771   Graduated. "The Rising Glory of America" by Hugh Henry Brackenridge and Freneau read by Brackenridge at the ceremonies.

1772   First publications—"The Rising Glory of America" and *The American Village*.

1775   "American Liberty" and other first poems about the events of the Revolutionary War.

1776   July—Hessians land on Long Island; Freneau had left for West Indies.

1778   Returned to New Jersey; in July, joined the New Jersey Militia.

1779   Contributed to Brackenridge's *United States Magazine*.

1780   Imprisoned on a British prison ship in New York harbor.

1781   Published "The British Prison Ship" and began association with the Philadelphia *Freeman's Journal:* occasional poems on the events of the war.

1786   Publication of *The Poems of Philip Freneau*.

1787   Publication of *A Journey from Philadelphia to New York*.

1788   Washington named president. Publication of *The Miscellaneous Works of Mr. Philip Freneau*.

1790   Married; connected with the New York *Daily Advertiser*.

1791   Established the *National Gazette* in Philadelphia.

1792   Freneau, as editor of the *National Gazette*, accused of being Thomas Jefferson's tool.

1793   The Genet affair. Death of the *National Gazette*.

1794   Established own press in Mount Pleasant, New Jersey; published *The Monmouth Almanac*.

1795   Printed on his own press *Poems Written between the Years 1768 & 1794;* began the *Jersey Chronicle*.

1796 · John Adams elected, *Jersey Chronicle* dies.
1797　Began editing the New York *Time Piece, and Literary Companion.*
1798　In debt; left the *Time Piece.*
1799　Began series of letters to Philadelphia *Aurora* signed Robert Slender; collected them in *Letters on Various Interesting and Important Subjects.*
1800　Jefferson elected president.
1802　Freneau returned to the sea.
1809　Publication of *Poems Written and Published during the American Revolutionary War.*
1815　Publication of *A Collection of Poems Chiefly on American Affairs.*
1822　A series of essays, "Recollections of Past Times and Events," printed in the Trenton *True American.*
1832　Freneau died December 18, aged eighty.

CHAPTER 1

Heritage

PHILIP MORIN FRENEAU, poet and essayist of Revolutionary America, is a complex figure. He was a propagandist for country and party, but he believed that art should be valued even if it were not utilitarian. He was a patriot, but he enjoyed the advantages of other lands. He was a man who prided himself on his occupation as sea captain, but he also wrote of the beauties of a rural retreat. He often altered his style and philosophy as he encountered new styles and new philosophies, but his values changed little from those of his college years. He began life as the son of a trader and man of property, became one himself, and added to these duties the interests of a gentleman of the Enlightenment. His pride lay in his poetry, but he was also proud of being more than a poet. He lived in an exciting age, and he participated actively in that excitement. He and his works are all the more interesting because one cannot easily classify them—or him.

Philip's heritage, which provided him with a family seat and with a wide circle of relatives, assured him stability in the often chaotic age of the American Revolution. His father's family first came to the American colonies in 1705, and it was led by Andre Fresneau (Philip was the first to alter the spelling of the last name). Andre became a member in good standing of the closely knit New York Huguenot community, was an elder in the French Huguenot church, and in 1710, married Marie Morin of a prominent New York family. The Fresneau eldest son (also Andre) and his brother Pierre (Philip's father) carried on the family Bordeaux and Madeira wine trade.

Pierre Fresneau was the traveler for the firm, and consequently he must have told his son many tales of foreign lands. Pierre, who made Madeira the seat of his operations, procured the wine and shipped it to various parts of the colonies. On one of his trips to make his collections in New Jersey, he married Agnes Watson, the daughter of a prosperous New Jersey landed family; and he thus became the first of his family to marry outside the Huguenot community. Pierre continued in the wine business, although he and his wife settled in New York. There, on January 2, 1752 (O.S.), Philip Morin, the eldest of his five children, was born. Business must have been good, for Pierre bought that same year a thousand-acre estate in Monmouth County, New Jersey, where he built his residence, named Mount Pleasant. Although Pierre sailed back to Madeira, he returned in 1753 to settle down at Mount Pleasant and to enter the dry goods trade. Thereafter, he worked in New Jersey and in New York City.

We have little factual knowledge about Philip Freneau's early education. He may have had his first lessons at home, since the family books still extant show an educated taste. Among these books are the Bible, books of sermons and catechisms, and volumes of Joseph Addison and Alexander Pope, authors later treasured by Philip. Family tradition holds that at an early age he was sent to a boarding school in New York, where he, although removed from his immediate family, would probably have been under the surveillance of his Fresneau relatives in the city. He probably entered a school in New York which offered a curriculum similar to that of the Princeton grammar school, which taught Latin, Graeco-Roman maps, and geography; one hour a day was devoted to writing and arithmetic; and a weekly exercise was "reading the English authors with propriety and grace," with special attention being paid to grammar and spelling.[1]

When Philip was fifteen, he was sent to a Latin school at Penolopen, New Jersey, to prepare for college. The school was directed by the Reverend Alexander Mitchell, who was closely connected with Princeton: his tutoring was effective, for Freneau was admitted directly to the Princeton sophomore class, having satisfied the requirements expected of freshmen. Before he was to enter, however, in October, 1767, his father died; and we can imagine the turmoil of the home, and the reexamination of the plans for the future by Pierre Fresneau's family. Fortunately, Philip's education was not halted—his family's wishes evidently were strong that he enter college instead of being placed in the business of one of the family's relatives. And so, in the fall of 1768, one year after his father's death, Philip Freneau entered the College of New Jersey, now Princeton.

I   *College and Early Literary Attempts*

Freneau's college experiences and experiments made a lasting impression on his life and later activities. Like many other students, he gained more than the knowledge imparted in class. He learned about the life in, and the politics of, other colonies; for students from New England, the Carolinas, Virginia, and Georgia as well as from the Middle States attended the College of New Jersey. The college town also offered the advantage of being on the Philadelphia-New York post road, and it boasted a newsshop, where the latest political pamphlets were to be purchased, read, and studied. Then, too, eminent colonial politicians visited the college to speak to the students or to be honored by them. Thus Princeton, although far from being a Boston, New York, or Philadelphia, had close ties nevertheless with all three and was by no means a backwater.

In 1768, the year Freneau entered, the College of New Jersey installed a president who was to be responsible for much of the distinction gained by the college. John Witherspoon had been summoned from Scotland by the New York and Philadelphia Presbyterians to head the college and to lead the colonial church. His immediate duties on his arrival were the revision of the college curriculum and the raising of money. To stimulate contributions, he traveled in all of the colonies, where he preached, discussed the educational need for the College of New Jersey and its material requirements, and recruited students. At that time, he was one of the most well-traveled men in the colonies, another circumstance that discouraged a provincial bias at Princeton. He introduced to the college the study of philosophy and the study of a modern language (French, although the students later discovered that his Scots accent was not similar to that of Paris), as well as history and oratory; and insisted on his students' mastering the English language. The students under his tutelege were thus well equipped to take part in the political and social debates of the day.

Despite Witherspoon's strict theological stand, students found him to be compassionate, and they revered him long after they had left college. In one of his later poems, Freneau describes this "*Caledonian* Sage":

> His words still vibrate on my ear
> His precepts, solemn and severe,
> Alarmed the vicious, and the base,
> To virtue gave the loveliest face
> That human-kind can wear.[2]

We should keep in mind that the president was a constant presence at the college and that prayers and sermons were as much a part of the curriculum as the other studies that Witherspoon described in 1772:

In the first year they read Latin and Greek, with the Roman and Grecian antiquities, and Rhetoric. In the second, continuing the study of the languages, they learn the first principles of Philosophy, and the elements of mathematical knowledge. The third, though the languages are not wholly omitted, is chiefly employed in Mathematics and Natural Philosophy and going through a course of Moral Philosophy. In addition to these, the President gives lectures to the juniors and seniors, which consequently every student hears twice over in his course, first, upon Chronology and History, and afterwards upon Composition and Criticism. He has also been taught the French language last winter, and it will continue to be taught to all who desire to learn it.[3]

With the exception of French, there were probably no electives; but the curriculum was a liberal one. From the evidence available, Freneau paid most attention to history, composition, and criticism. Of the classic authors, Witherspoon praised Cicero, Quintilian, Homer and Lucian; then he recommended study of Addison, Jonathan Swift, Pope, William Shakespeare, John Donne, Miguel de Cervantes, John Milton, Andrew Marvell, Bernard le Bouvier de Fontenelle and Nicholas Boileau—authors offering a wide range of styles and attitudes.

Of all authors, Freneau seems to have selected Horace and Pope for his favorites—his annotations of them indicate that Witherspoon discussed the lives of the poets to inculcate morality in the students. We do not know how Freneau ranked in his class; we know only that he did graduate. We also know that he was equipped to continue in later life his reading in the classics and in philosophy and that he knew French (whether acquired in college or not). But Freneau's learning, as demonstrated in his later works, was less important than the attitudes and interests which he and his fellow students maintained the rest of their lives. These students of the College of New Jersey of Freneau's generation had cultivated the habit of inquiry which was demonstrated by their interest in diverse aspects of the life they saw around them and in new theories and new knowledge. The men educated at Princeton were not dogmatists.

Freneau also gained much from extracurricular activities at Princeton. There was a certain amount of cordiality between town and gown; there was the village tavern; and there were village maids to enjoy. Freneau recalled wintertime skating and strolls when students "closed our Books, forgot our cares,/ To stray where *Rocky Mountain* rears/ His weather-beaten crest."[4] During the vacations, students also relaxed. But, one legend, which relates that Freneau's fellow student James Madison visited him during these vacations, is proved inaccurate by a letter from Freneau to Madison, written shortly after graduation: "While I was at College I had but a short participation of your agreeable friendship and the few persons I converse with and yet fewer, whose conversation I delight in make me regret the Loss of it."[5] But such vacations probably enabled Freneau to invite to his home other students for a period of closer companionship.

During the college term, however, extracurricular frivolity was likely to be cut short by the college authorities and, in times of religious enthusiasm, by the other students. In June, 1770, the celebrated preacher George Whitefield spoke to the students of Princeton; and, if Freneau did not hear him, he probably heard other such traveling preachers. But sermons were not the only form of entertainment for students, for John Witherspoon initiated at Princeton another form of educational entertainment—orations by students, who apparently had free choice of subject—and the student audience had just as much freedom to express opinions of the orator. Freneau, in a poem entitled "The Distrest Orator," describes one Archibald, who, "six weeks, and more, he tax'd his brain,/ And wrote petitions to the Muses"—only to have his memory fail him. But Archibald started his oration well—" 'I talk'd of *custom*, *fame*, and *fashion*,/ Of *moral evil* and *compassion*' "—but forgot the rest: " 'I gap'd once more,/ And set the audience in a roar,/ They laugh'd me out of face.' " But help could come from former students, as shown by a letter from William Paterson to Aaron Burr: "Be pleased to accept of the enclosed notes on *dancing*. If you pitch upon it as the subject of your next discourse,they may, perhaps, furnish you with a few hints, and enable you to compose with the greater facility and despatch."[6] Unfortunately, Freneau's student orations, along with so many of his other papers, have been lost.

The literary clubs offered the students a less formal and less public opportunity to air their compositions. When Freneau attended Princeton, two clubs, the Whig Society and the Cliosophic Society, rivaled each other for the number of honors their members could gain. Despite the name "Whig," and the Whigs' habit of calling the members of Clio, Tories, the clubs were not separated according to political principle, unless it were that of collegiate politics. The Whig Society had in its ranks such wits as Freneau, Hugh Henry Brackenridge, James Madison, and William Bradford; the Clios included Samuel Springer, Aaron Burr, and, occasionally, an alumnus, William Paterson. The nature of the literary exercises of these clubs is indicated by Paterson: "I used to curse anathematise the poetical conundrums, epigrams, squibs, etc., of our Nassovian Bards. But I find they make as good musick as their neighbors: whether they have more common sense, is a moot point."[7] During the 1770–71 term, the two clubs directed their literary output against each other in a "paper" war.

Of this "paper" war, we still have some of the Whigs' artillery, preserved by William Bradford—poems by Brackenridge, Freneau, and Madison. During this war Freneau practiced the poetic satire and the invective which later made him infamous—one of his poems begins, "Hail worthy Sages, sprung from dust and dirt,/ With Scandal cloathed, besides a lousy shirt."[8] But even Madison's verses are not written in a more elevated style; for one of his, entitled "A Poem Against the Tories," contains these lines:

> Come noble whigs, disdain these sons
> Of screech owls, monkeys, & baboons
> Keep up you[r] minds to humourous themes
> And verdant meads & flowing streams
> Untill this tribe of dunces find
> The baseness of their grovelling mind
> And skulk within their dens together
> Where each ones stench will kill his brother.[9]

Although Freneau kept and later used some of his verses written during this war, publishing them as "McSwiggen," Madison but three short years later decided that such versification had to be abandoned: something more substantial was needed to occupy a mature adult's time. Fortunately, Freneau never reached such a conclusion.

Although probably not part of the "paper" war, "Father Bombo's Pilgrimage," a collaboration by Brackenridge and Freneau, seems to have been part of their literary society productions. Volume II was found among the papers of William Bradford, and volume I may have been written by earlier members of the club. "Father Bombo" is hailed by Brackenridge's biographer as being "the earliest example of American prose fiction,"[10] but what the manuscript demonstrates most clearly is the high good spirits of the two gentlemen who composed it. Brackenridge, who wrote the first chapter of the second volume, guides the traveler Bombo through various misadventures which include his being taken prisoner by a French privateer and then by an Irish ship. From it, he is thrown overboard in a hogshead.

The parts initialed by Freneau demonstrate not only high spirits but also the broad satire and the melancholy poetry so often found in his later work. Freneau's part begins with Bombo still in possession of his cask and once more at sea, but he soon lands in Ireland and applies for a job as a schoolmaster. He is examined by the board on Latin, Greek, anatomy, natural philosophy and metaphysics and has to write a declamation on the spot. Bombo's ignorance and self-assurance prevail over the ignorance of the trustees, as in this section of his examination on anatomy:"—in the next place said Patrick, how do you find the number of nails a person has? By multiplying the means and Extremes together and dividing the Quotient by the answer said I; Very well, said he and how many do you find them to be? Four and twenty, said I, including the Thumb nails. This they agreed was right."[11]

After Bombo is given the school, he spends his time delivering floggings until the students protest, bind him on a cow, and then tie him to a tree. After this experience, Bombo resolves to quit Ireland for Scotland, but first he composes a song that begins in the accepted melancholy manner:

> But what has Love to do with me
> Unknown ashore, distressed by Sea,
> Now hast'ning to the Tomb;
> Whilst here I rove, and pine, and weep,
> Sav'd from the fury of the deep
> To find alas on shore a harder doom.

Soon, however, Bombo's song concentrates on the one ill he finds the hardest to bear, the lack of food: "Ah cease my Song and oaten flute/ Be thou, my voice forever mute/ My Stomach tells me I can sing no more."

The third chapter, also by Freneau, is much weaker than the first two; it reads as if the author were anxious to have Bombo complete his journeys and return home. Freneau quickly transports Bombo to Scotland, London, France, Rome, and then to Mecca, the goal of his journey, from whence he returns home via Cadiz and Madeira. After Bombo finally arrives at Philadelphia, he goes to the "Castle," probably Princeton itself. The authors conclude the third chapter with a general warning: ". . . let no person be so bold as to write any Second or third parts to this History as we now declare it is compleated as much as it ever will be. Our Sage Hero has undergone toils sufficient to kill any common man and we now leave him whether he is to fly on the Wings of Fame or sink in eternal obscurity—Finis."

Certainly volume II of "Father Bombo's Pilgrimage" was not intended as a serious literary exercise. It was probably intended to entertain the members of the literary club with its satire on the college and collegians. Students named specifically by the manuscript are Joshua Hart, John Smith and Nathan Perkins, all members of the Cliosophic Society. Bombo himself, with his identifying red wig, may be Brackenridge's and Freneau's satiric treatment of yet another member of Clio. The literary clubs gave fledgling authors an appreciative audience—one especially appreciative, we suspect, when the wit was directed against the opposing club.

Freneau's collegiate productions also include a handful of poems that are unconnected with the rivalry between the two literary clubs. Since many of them are derivative, the poems may have been inspired by his readings for class; some may even have been responses to specific assignments; a few may have been read at club meetings. Generally, they reflect neoclassic values and the neoclassic emphasis on the importance of history in the search for universal rules. Although Freneau in later political and literary battles often ignored the general and universal in favor of the specific and individual, he does not do so in his collegiate poems. If he celebrates an individual, that individual is likely to be biblical or historical, and the tale is told to illustrate a universal truth. Such is one of Freneau's earliest poems, "The History of the Prophet Jonah" (1768), which Freneau attempted in couplets and which merely follows the biblical story.

A historical poem, "Columbus to Ferdinand," is more interesting in that Freneau gives his own interpretation of a historical event. The poem is cast as Columbus' speech to Ferdinand; and in it he begs permission to depart on his voyage of exploration. Columbus neglects the plea of adventure and exploration for their own sakes; Freneau has him argue only from reason. Columbus pictures the possibility that the other half of the earth is only water, but he counters: " 'Tis reason's voice that bids me think not so,/ I think more nobly of the Almighty hand.' " Columbus is well enough read in the classics to quote Seneca's prophecy of the discovery of remote regions; he is not fearful of the elements because, " 'Reason shall steer, and shall disarm the gale.' " In Columbus' (and Freneau's) universe, nothing is done in vain: nature would not have revealed to man the compass if he were not fated to wander from his native habitat. To us, such reasoning by Columbus seems incongruous; to Freneau, the story was undoubtedly another proof of the eternal laws of Reason.

Freneau chose another basic and eternal theme in writing about the love of Sappho for Phaon, but in this poem, "The Monument of Phaon," less emphasis is placed on reason and moderation; for more is given to the pathetic and melancholic. When Sappho hears of Phaon's faithlessness and of his death in a foreign land, she denounces him but cannot deny the strength of her love:

> "I charge thee, Phaon, by this deed of woe
> To meet me in the Elysian shades below,
> No rival beauty shall pretend a share,
> Sappho alone shall walk with Phaon there."

The poem ends dramatically when Sappho leaps into the sea. "The Monument of Phaon" imitates the popular poetry of the pre-Romantics, sharing with it the increasing emphasis on landscape and wild passions.

"The Pyramids of Egypt" is also imitative of another popular theme in its tale of the destructive power of Time. The poem consists of a dialogue in unrhymed verse between a Traveller, a Genius, and Time. Genius, to emphasize the great age of the pyramids, makes frequent historical allusions; thus, Freneau

conforms to that neoclassic ideal. But Genius also speaks as if of the
Graveyard School as he describes the tombs within the pyramids:

> " 'Tis darkness all, with hateful silence join'd—
> Here drowsy bats enjoy a dull repose,
> And marble coffins, vacant of their bones,
> Show where the royal dead in ruin lay!"

Although Time boasts of his ability to destroy the pyramids (com-
paring them rather infelicitously to "dwindled warts" upon the
earth's body), Freneau is not grieving over the power of Time to
destroy; for Time also admonishes the Traveller, "There's nought
but God immortal—He alone/ Exists secure." In these college
poems, Freneau not only was experimenting with various styles of
verse but also was wandering among various explanations of universal law.

Among the college poems which deal more directly with contemporary manners, "The Adventures of Simon Swaugum, A Village Merchant" illustrates Freneau's satiric bent. The poem, also
dated 1768, is good in its realistic descriptions of the life of a small
farmer. Simon, the farmer, decides for no very good reason to set up
a store in the country, which he loves, again for no very apparent
reason:

> And yet no splendid objects there were seen,
> No distant hills, in gaudy colours clad,
> Look where you would, the prospect was but mean,
> Scrub oaks, and scatter'd pines, and willows sad—
> Banks of a shallow river, stain'd with mud;
> A stream, where never swell'd the tide of flood.

Simon's trip to the city to buy his goods is also realistically told: he
seeks out the cheapest stores, and the merchants welcome him—
until his money runs out. On Simon's way home, some of his goods
are broken; at home, his neighbors declare his prices too high.
Finally, when poor Simon gives up his venture by charging no profit
at all, his shelves are cleared and a puncheon of rum is quickly
drunk by his neighbors.

Freneau also presents a realistic story in "Epitaph on the
Tombstone of Patrick Bay." The speaker in the poem, Patrick
himself, does not mourn either the power of Time or the inevitable

decay of all things. Instead, the poem is a complaint by Patrick that "Not Fate or Death,—but doctor Rowe/ Advanc'd to give the deadly blow/ That smote me to the shades below." These two poems are the liveliest; but "Simon Swaugum" is the most original of Freneau's collegiate productions. However, these poems (together with "The Citizen's Resolve" and "The Power of Fancy," to be considered later) are illustrative of much of his later work. In them we see his reliance upon the styles and subject matter of the accepted English poets, but we also see, although perhaps too rarely, his ability to picture the habits and manners of those around him and to hold them up for mockery. In few of the poems is there intense personal emotion, despite his attempt in several of them to evoke emotion by use of the pathetic. The theme of mourning the passage of time, which many find so interesting in his later works, is not yet dominant, although it is occasionally found. At this time, Freneau was experimenting with the contradictory themes of reason and emotion, both of which are present in what may be his best collegiate poem, "The Rising Glory of America."

But "The Rising Glory of America," a joint labor of Freneau and Brackenridge, also testifies to the rising colonial patriotic feeling which was also present on the campus. Because the Stamp Act required a two-pound tax for matriculation and for graduation, students at the colleges were directly affected by Parliament's unpopular acts. And, naturally, the students followed closely the tentative motions of the colonies toward united action as indicated by the nonimportation agreements. 1770 was an active political year for the students. In July the merchants lifted the nonimportation ban on everything but tea, which was regarded as a betrayal of the cause. The letter from the merchants, informing others of their decision, was burned by a hangman hired for the occasion by the students; it was burned "with hearty Wishes, that the Names of all Promoters of such a daring Breach of Faith, may be blasted in the Eyes of every Lover of Liberty, and their Names handed down to Posterity, as Betrayers of their Country."[12]

The protests of the students were institutionalized to some extent by the graduation ceremonies held during these years. In September, 1768, these theses were defended at the ceremonies: "It is the Interest of any Nation, to have the Trade of its new Countries, as free from Embarrassments as possible," and "It is lawful for every Man, and in many Cases, his indispensable Duty, to hazard his Life in defence of his Civil Liberty." But in the graduation ceremonies of 1771, Freneau's part was merely to argue in favor of the ancients on the question, "Does ancient Poetry excel the modern?" Since he was "necessarily absent," his remarks were read by another student. The seventh item on the agenda was apparently the patriotic highlight of the program: "A Poem, on *The rising glory of America*' was spoken by Mr. Brackenridge, and received with great applause by the Audience."[13]

Although well received, "The Rising Glory of America" has neither a striking style nor an unusual subject matter to recommend it: it is not a poem of Romantic fancy or of Revolutionary fervor. The poets felt obligated to confine themselves to historical fact, and they had to forego giving free rein to their fancy. They did, however, concern themselves with a current philosophical-poetical concept about the inevitable westward movement of empires and arts. Freneau and Brackenridge describe what can be done and what is being done—that the impetus is shifting to the West and will continue to do so. Thus, although not a Revolutionary poem, "The Rising Glory" did nothing to lessen the confidence of Americans that the way of the world demanded their greatness.

The philosophical justification for the title is clearly presented. The beginning speaker traces the passage of glory from Memphis, to Greece, to Rome, then to Britain and declares: "A Theme more new, tho' not less noble, claims/ Our ev'ry thought on this auspicious day;/ The rising glory of this western world." To the poets, it is historically inevitable that glory should continue her drive westward. Other sections of the poem also support this theme, as when the poets predict the Muses' move to America, encouraging a new Homer, a new Milton, a new Pope. Commerce and Science are already firmly rooted in the new land; greater things will come. The poets see all aspects of greatness linked together. Commerce owes her growth to science, and science, to liberty: "sweet liberty!/ Without whose aid the noblest genius fails,/ And science irretrievably must die."

But, in their praise of commerce, science, and liberty, the poets do not forget the ideal life as presented by other poets of the time—the virtuous rural life. They show its advocates through history and then depict North America's life as more virtuous than that of South America, for agriculture, unlike life in the mines, gives serenity: "such the joys/ And such the fate of those whom heav'n hath bless'd/

With souls enamour'd of a country life." Such virtue evidently does not go unrewarded, for the poets look far into the future and regard the Millenium, with its "joys too divine/ For fallen man to know":

> Such days the world
> And such, America, thou first shall have
> When ages yet to come have run their round
> And future years of bliss alone remain.

The concept of progress places the golden age in the future, and the poets endorse this placement both theologically and philosophically.

The concept of progress was often allied with that of primitivism and with emphasis on the value of innate feelings, and both concepts join in the idea of the "noble savage." For the two graduates, however, the "noble savage" does not exist. They discuss the origin of the Indians and present many hypotheses, but the graduates select none and declare the whole question a maze. And, while they mourn for the Indians, they do so because the Indians "wander'd blindfold down the steep of time/ . . . To them fair science never op'd her stores,/ Nor sacred truth sublim'd the soul to God." This view represents both the neoclassic and theological viewpoints. Later in the poem, when discussing the French and Indian War, the poets present a stronger view of the Indian as "the savage race,/ Unstable as the sea, wild as the winds,/ Cruel as death, and treacherous as hell." These lines may have been contributed by frontiersman Brackenridge, for they are omitted in Freneau's 1786 rendering of the poem.

Indeed, to compare Freneau's 1786 "Rising Glory" to that published in 1772 by both poets is interesting. In an introductory note to his revision, Freneau declares his changes: "such parts being only inserted here as were written by the author of this volume. A few more modern lines towards the conclusion are incorporated with the rest, being a supposed prophetical anticipation of subsequent events." Freneau probably deleted Brackenridge's lines, but he changed more than the prophecy toward the end. The most noticeable change is the deletion of all favorable references to Britain; other changes include less emphasis on religion, the alteration of names of heroes, and the omission of events which were fresh in the mind in 1772 but had become less memorable in 1786.

In the poem of 1772, the poets turn from South America to North,

"Discover'd by Britannia for her sons," where, on the frontier, "the
British standard awes the coward host." Although the Indians are
cruel, "The British Epithet is merciful:/ And we the sons of Britain
learn like them/ To conquer and to spare." Peace has come, for
"Britannia holds the empire of the waves,/ And welcomes ev'ry bold
adventurer/ To view the wonders of old Ocean's reign." And, in the
future, the hope is that "Britain's sons shall spread/ Dominion to the
north and south and west/ Far from th'Atlantic to Pacific shores." All
these lines are omitted in Freneau's 1786 edition; but, though we do
not know which of the two poets composed the lines, it was appropriate to omit them in 1786.

In a similar vein, the passages honoring Generals Braddock and
Johnson are deleted, and one in praise of Washington is inserted. In
1786, Christopher Columbus alone is pictured as a discoverer: in
1772, John Cabot and Sir Walter Raleigh (whose virtues "pour new
lustre on Britannia's isle") share the honor. The 1772 poem reflects
the still widely held view of the colonists as good subjects of the
English king and as good "sons of Britain." Also indicative of the
changing times, or of Freneau's change, is the lesser emphasis on
religion in the 1786 version; for no longer is America described as "a
land where the more noble light/ Of holy revelation beams." And,
while Freneau in 1772 saw that in the future, "we too shall boast/
Our Alexanders, Pompeys, heroes, kings," the immense change
brought about by the American Revolution caused Freneau's alteration to read, "we too shall boast/ Our Scipios, Solons, Catos,
sages, chiefs."

The original poem, perhaps because of its two authors, is uneven
in both style and thought; but it illustrates the truths which the
poets accepted at the time: the idea of progress moving westwards,
the theological truths, the allegiance to Britain and the high praise
paid reason and science. It is, in fact, a guide to the minds of
Americans in 1772.

We do not know why Freneau did not attend the graduation
ceremonies, but we do know that his years spent at Princeton were
good ones for him. The college curriculum and atmosphere gave
him the opportunity to study closely modern and ancient poets and
to experiment with their styles. His poetry of the college years
shows his imitation of style and content: reason is praised, and mild
melancholy is honored. But we also see in these poems a less derivative aspect in the satiric touches Freneau gave to even the most

melancholy poems as well as to those portraying contemporary manners. There are extant from this period no political poems; for although students were concerned with current reactions to British policy, Freneau had not yet begun commenting poetically on such events. In fact, from study of "The Rising Glory of America," we conclude that he and Brackenridge felt just as they ought as British subjects. But the satiric political poems were soon to come.

II *Years of Indecision: First Published Poetry*

The years between Freneau's graduation from college in the fall of 1771 and the outbreak of hostilities in early 1776 are marked by his restlessness. We have reports of him in Philadelphia, New York City, Maryland, Long Island, Princeton, and back home at Mount Pleasant. Although he published his first poetry, he also taught school, may have studied law, did study theology, and is rumored to have taken berth as a mate on a ship. At this point, he was not a dedicated poet; but he did publish "The Rising Glory of America" and a collection of his own poetry, and he cheerfully accepted their poor reception. He was not a consistent propagandist either, for he ignored the growing revolutionary sentiment in the colonies until 1775 when he poured his satire upon General Gage, as did John Trumbull in *M'Fingal*. But Freneau's dedication to politics did not last long; and he sailed early in 1776, perhaps because of his restlessness, to the West Indies. Certainly Freneau was not the "poet of the Revolution" in its beginning stages.

F. L. Pattee's remark that "the period between 1772 and 1775 is at best a vague one in our life of the poet"[14] is true. Of the year 1771 we know only two facts: that he was not at graduation and that his mother remarried on June 5, 1771. Because of a letter Freneau wrote to Madison, we do know about some of his activities of 1772. Early in the year he had undertaken a school at Flatbush in Long Island, and in April he had seen Madison. Since Madison was visiting Bradford in Philadelphia in April, a reunion there of at least three of the Whig Society may have occurred. Freneau, who returned to Flatbush, soon left, swearing, "the youth of that detested place, are void of reason and of grace." As he tells the story to Madison, "I luckily escaped with my goods to Princetown, where I remained till commencement." Although he doesn't mention it to Madison, he also published in Philadelphia during the summer "The Rising Glory of America." When he reports the publication of

The American Village in New York, he adds casually that, "as to the main poem, it is damned by all good and judicious Judges"; but Freneau is nevertheless pleased to announce that his name was on the title page. His next recounted movement is his arrival at the Somerset Academy in Maryland on October 18 to be Brackenridge's assistant teacher until the following October. Liking his new position no more than the previous one, he positively states that "this is the last time I shall enter into such a business."[15]

From the same letter, we learn a little about Freneau's hopes and leisure-time activities. He reports that he is busy writing a satire about "certain vicious persons of quality in N.Y.—who have also used me ill"—but that he is also composing pastorals. He started reading "physic," in case he "must turn quack." But his preference for a career is indicated: "I would go over for the gown this time two years, but the old hag necessity has got such a prodigious gripe of me that I fear I shall never be able to accomplish it." "Going over for the gown" is explained by a letter from William Bradford to Madison, dated December 25, 1773: "Mr Breckingridge is well & still in Maryland. Mr Freneau passed thro' here a few days ago but I could not get a sight of him. He intends sailing next spring for England to take Orders."[16] Although Freneau never attained this goal, he was seriously studying theology in 1773 and 1774.

Freneau may have finished his term in his hated job at the Somerset Academy by October, 1773. Bradford's letter places Freneau in Philadelphia in December, but we do not know where he was coming from or going to. Perhaps family affairs had called him back to New Jersey, for his stepfather had died less than two years after his marriage, and his mother may have needed him. That Freneau was still considering additional study in England at the end of 1773 shows his unconcern for current events, for a furor was rising in all the colonies because of the retention of the Townshend duties on tea and the favoritism shown the East India Company. In New York and Philadelphia, the Whigs were successful in getting agents of the company to resign and the public to boycott tea; but they were less successful in Boston, where, on December 16, 1773, the Tea Party occurred. Freneau knew of the furor, for he wrote "Margery and Patty, A Boston Dialogue," a light poem, in which Patty convinces Margery she must not drink tea. But Freneau may have thought, like many of the colonists, that the trouble would be short-lived.

Contrary to the hopes of many in both England and America, the trouble was not soon over. On March 31, 1774, Parliament revealed the Boston Port Act, which closed the city to all shipping. In May and June, more "Intolerable Acts" were imposed, ones affecting not only Boston but all of Massachusetts. In July, 1774, Parliament passed the Quebec Act, which called for direct taxation of Canada by Parliament and which officially established the Catholic Church there. This second provision raised fears of an established church in the colonies, and once more large segments of the population were hostile to King George III and Parliament. The acts united all the colonies, and they called for a Continental Congress, which met in September and October of that fall. This Congress, which denied any desire for independence, restated its loyalty to the king; but it also declared a boycott of goods from Great Britain, Ireland, and the British West Indies. Nonimportation was to go into effect on December 1, 1774; nonexportation, on September 10, 1775.[17]

Of Freneau and his actions during this exciting year of 1774 we know little. He may have attended the meeting of the Presbyterian synod in Philadelphia in May, but May is also the last date that appears in Freneau's theological notebook; he gave up the study soon afterward. He dated one of his poems, "Pictures of Columbus," 1774; but this work has no reference to current events and was not published until later. Perhaps he was wise in withholding publication; he probably would have met the same fate as his fellow poet Brackenridge, who during this year published "Divine Revelation." Even Freneau's fellow Whig Bradford had to confess that "I am afraid he has published it at an improper time; the political storm is too high for the soft still voice of the muse to be listened to; & indeed this does not seem the proper time for poetry unless it be such as Tyrtaeus wrote."[18] And Madison replied, "The same merit in a Political or humorous Composition would have rung the Author's fame through every province in the Continent."[19] But Freneau, like Brackenridge, was not yet ready for political poetry.

In 1772, when Freneau published his volume of poetry, events had not yet demanded stern poetry, and Bradford had welcomed *The American Village*. In writing to Madison, he said, "I would send you the poem had I an opportunity! It is well worthy your perusal."[20] Few would be as generous as Bradford, for the major and title poem, "The American Village," is awkwardly planned and organized. The poet hops from subject to subject with very little transition. According to Lewis Leary,[21] "The American Village" owes much to Pope's "Windsor Forest"; but, whereas Pope's unifying principle was the forest itself, Freneau declines to limit himself to one location. He shifts the scene from the village to an imaginary island, to the banks of the Hudson, to the environs of Hudson's Bay. When Pope praises rural occupations, recounts his legend of the nymph, praises the Thames, and hails the coming of peace, he grounds each subject in the area of Windsor Forest—and thus achieves a more unified poem than Freneau. While Freneau follows Pope in the subjects discussed, his attitude toward them often differs from Pope's, thus illustrating the change in poetic ideals from Pope's reason to Freneau's sentiment. For instance, Pope describes the ancient times as being harsh and miserable: "The Swain with Tears his frustrate Labour yields,/ And famish'd dies amidst his ripen'd Fields." The land itself was "A dreary Desart and a gloomy Waste,/ To Savage Beasts and Savage Laws a Prey."[22] But in Freneau's view, natural man, left alone to grow by himself on the island removed from the rest of the world, would have been completely happy:

> Small fields had then suffic'd, and grateful they,
> The annual labours of his hands to pay;
> And free his right to search the briny flood
> For fish, or slay the creatures of the wood.[23]

Freneau warns his readers, "Nor think this mighty land of old contain'd/ The plund'ring wretch, or man of bloody mind." The natives were free in their paradise until "rav'nous nations with industrious toil,/ Conspired to rob them of their native soil:/ Then bloody wars, and death and rage arose."

Also indicative of the changing poetic taste are two legends. Pope creates a Greek myth for Windsor forest: his nymph, when pursued by Pan, appeals to Diana and Cynthia for succor. Freneau's legend tells of Colma and Caffraro, two lovers, whose canoe meets disaster while they are on a trading expedition. The two are noble savages, whose deeds and virtues are "fit to rival GREEK or ROMAN fame." The legend, especially Colma's vision of life after death, anticipates both Freneau's later Indian poems and the ones questioning the nature of the afterlife. Here, Freneau speculates whether the two lovers departed to the sun, to Acheron, or to the Christian heaven, "or if return'd to dread nihility,/ You'll still be happy, for. you will not be."

Pope and Freneau, naturally, also have different views of the world political scene. For Pope, Britain's glory still lies in the future. Although Freneau, as in "The Rising Glory of America," still predicts "yet shall this land with rising pomp divine,/ In it's own splendor and Britannia's shine," he nevertheless sees "the golden season now from BRITAIN fled." America is the last land to receive greatness for the simple reason that "no other regions latent yet remain." If, therefore, like Rome and Britain, America falls to decay, "the world itself must fall as well as she."

But the poet in Freneau's poem is less concerned with world affairs than with his own peace of mind. Rid of "pedantic labours," he looks to a life in his village, where "heaven born contemplation shall be mine"; but such descriptions of idyllic retreats are often found in Freneau's early verse. While the very early "On Retirement" was not included in the 1772 volume, it, too, imitates Pope as well as the American Churchill. But, unlike Pope's "On Solitude," "On Retirement" lectures man: "vain, foolish man! how vast thy pride,/ How little can your wants supply!" The poet is superior, for all he desires is "a cottage I could call my own." "The Farmer's Winter Evening" in *The American Village*, also contains the theme of the idyllic retreat, but Freneau, not content with just one fashionable theme, also presents the theme of the superiority of night:

> But thou, O night, with sober charms,
> Shall clasp me in thy sable arms.
> For thee I love the winter eve,
> The noisy day for thee I leave.

And Freneau did not omit the theme of love. The dedication reads, "To the NYMPH I never saw," and the poet confesses that "Love hath my mind in shackles kept." Could the poet dwell with "my pretty rural shepherdess," "all ARCADIA should be mine." Although in celebrating love, night, and country retirement the poem follows the poetic fashions of the day, it follows too many of them, which results in a lack of unity.

For the 1786 edition of his poems, Freneau reworked "The Farmer's Winter Evening" and retitled it "The Citizen's Resolve."

In the revision, the praise of night is shortened, the emphasis upon the nymph is lessened, and the commendation of country life is strengthened. Freneau now has the longing for a rural retreat spoken by Lysander, who wishes "dull Commerce, hence, with all thy train/ Of debts, and dues, and loss, and gain." The mention of Commerce permits the poet to furnish the revised poem with this surprise ending:

> So spoke Lysander, and in haste
> His clerks discharg'd, his goods re-cased,
> And to the western forests flew
> With fifty airy schemes in view;
> His ships were set to public sale—
> But what did all this change avail?—
> In three short months, sick of the heavenly train,
> In three short months—he moved to town again.

"The Farmer's Winter Evening" took very seriously the tradition of the pleasures of retirement in the country; but "The Citizen's Resolve" mocks that tradition, for Freneau now has a satiric attitude toward the idyllic life.

Freneau's satiric powers are represented in the 1772 *The American Village* by "The Miserable Life of a Pedagogue." Freneau's own experience—his detestation of his teaching jobs—no doubt furnished the subject, but his reading (perhaps of Pope's "Epistle to Dr. Arbuthnot") probably furnished the tone. The poem is a dramatic and humorous treatment of the persecution of the pedagogue by both students and parents. The profession "is certainly an arduous work,/ Enough to tire out Jew or Turk;/ And make a christian bite his nails." The persona, who had sworn never to have anything to do with such a job, found himself entangled "at a certain crazy season,/ When men have neither sense or reason." The students plague him by asking him questions "with sly design to know if I/Am vers'd in GRECIAN history," and their parents insist upon naming the knowledge their sons should gain. The persona concludes with a plague on the profession:

> Who'er to such a life is ty'd,
> Was born the day he should have dy'd;
> Born in an hour when angry spheres
> Were tearing caps, or pulling ears.

The language of the poem is easy and forceful; and the tone of the poem is consistent throughout, which is unusual for the poems in this volume or, indeed, for most of his early poems. Such shifts in mood are well illustrated by the last poem of the 1772 volume, "Upon a Very Ancient Dutch House on Long-Island." The poet envisages the old house as poetic, as made for "lone haunts and contemplation"; and he asks the reader to picture it when it was full of life, warmed with a cheerful fire, and occupied by a housewife and her husband who "snore full oft' the whole night out." We are also to picture the courtship of a swain and "some DUTCH lass, as thick as she was long." The swain pleads with the lass: "you alone shall soften all my care,/ My strong, my hearty, and industrious wife." But the poet soon recalls himself from this humor, and concludes his description in a more melancholy style:

> And none but me it's piteous fate lament,
> None, none but me o'er it's sad ashes mourn,
> Sent by the fates, and by APOLLO sent,
> To shed their latest tears upon it's silent urn.

When Freneau reworked this poem for publication in 1786, he omitted the snores and the description of the Dutch lass; and he also made the melancholy tone consistent throughout the poem. But, in improving the unity, Freneau robbed the poem of much of its interest and originality; and we must agree with some of the sentiments of the new closing lament: "None, none but I o'er its cold relics mourn,/ Sent by the muse—(the time perhaps misspent)—/To write dull stanzas on this dome forlorn."

The poems of *The American Village* are uneven in quality; indeed, only "The Miserable Life of a Pedagogue" shows the skill of his later, more famous poems. But the volume is, nevertheless, important because it shows Freneau's liking for variety—variety of theme, mood, and style. In these poems of 1772, Freneau has not dogmatically accepted any one philosophical truth (he was rarely to do so): he also appreciated variety in philosophy. Freneau's poetry of this time which was not included in *The American Village* but published later shows the same variety. While most of the poems not dealing with contemporary events concern eternal questions or historical events, Freneau varies widely in his style, tone, and even in his conclusions—for most of these poems are didactic.

In two uncollected poems, Freneau returned to a favorite college theme, the discovery of America. Although not published until later, "Discovery" was composed in 1772. It is a pessimistic poem, for the poet envisages man as plundering all the remote spots of the earth: "How few have sailed on virtue's nobler plan,/ How few with motives worthy of a man!" The discoverer's treatment of the natives is shameful: "Where'er they found a man they made a foe." And the poet advises the future explorer, "If wealth, or war, or science bid thee roam,/ Ah, leave religion and thy laws at home." But Freneau's picture of the natural man is inconsistent with his more realistic view in this and other poems, for he pictures the natives as sharing the same evil traits as the Europeans:

> Woes of their own those new found worlds invade,
> There, too, fierce passions the weak soul degrade,
>   *   *   *
> Revenge and death contending bosoms share,
> And pining envy claims her subjects there.

Perhaps these more cynical lines date from a later revision by a more cynical Freneau.

In "The Pictures of Columbus" of 1774, Freneau returns to the more accepted poetic view of a noble savage who lived in peace before the appearance of the white man. In Picture XIV, Columbus admires the newfound land: "All, all are free!—here God and nature reign;/ Their works unsullied by the hands of men." Because Freneau again mourns in this poem the evils brought to new lands by the explorers, his concept of Columbus has changed from the college poem "Columbus to Ferdinand." No longer is Columbus the strong man who argues his cause from historical truths and Reason's laws. This Columbus tries to persuade Isabella to fund the venture by playing on her avarice; he sketches for Ferdinand the picture of souls saved for the church; he tries to enlist men by creating visions of treasure. At the beginning of the poem, Freneau shows Columbus to be somewhat of a fanatic who will use any means available to gain his ends. After his discovery, Columbus becomes a figure who regrets his deed (temporarily): "We must away—enjoy your woods in peace,/ Poor, wretched, injur'd, harmless islanders." By the end of the poem, Freneau pictures him as fallen from the king's grace, alone and poor, a subject for pity and mourning, one who "liv'd to find new worlds for thankless kings."

The format of "The Pictures of Columbus" is good; for each of the eighteen pictures of the poem present a different aspect of Columbus' trials and discovery. Some pictures are dramatic dialogues, but others, more static and descriptive, are like the speech of the enchantress whom Columbus sought for her prediction:

> "The staring owl her note has sung;
> With gaping snakes my cave is hung;
> Of maiden hair my bed is made,
> Two winding sheets above it laid;
> With bones of men my shelves are pil'd
> And toads are for my supper boil'd;
> Three ghosts attend to fill my cup,
> And four to serve my pottage up;
> The crow is waiting to say grace:—
> Wouldst thou in such a dismal place
> The secrets of thy fortune trace?"

Such a marvelously Gothic picture is allowable—it does not disturb the unity of the whole—for it blends well with the picture in which it appears. Because of the shifting pictures, Freneau can show his versatility in painting the varied aspects of the man Columbus. Here the discoverer is unsure, there fanatical, here heroic, there pitiful: all moods can be pictured without disturbing the decorum of the poem.

In another poem from this period, Freneau is surer of the virtues of his title hero. "Epitaph of Peter Abelard: From the Latin" offers nothing but praise for Abelard, "Who conquer'd arts, who made all learning plain,/ And reach'd all knowledge, mortals can attain." The poem is somewhat of a surprise in that Freneau did not take advantage of the pathetic opportunities presented by the story of Eloisa and Abelard. Freneau does not neglect the pathetic, however, in his rendering of another ancient tale of star-crossed lovers, in "The Prayer of Orpheus." In another poem, "The Vernal Ague," Freneau, writing in the melancholy tradition, mourns because nature has lost its charms for him. In appealing to nature to help his condition, the poet introduces the traditional comparison of the seasons to the life of man: "Renew those colours, that must fade,/

When vernal suns forbear to roll,/ And endless winter chills the
soul." None of these poems are distinctively American, unless we
can consider the choice of Columbus as subject for Freneau's ambitious historical poem.

In a few poems, written during this period of experimentation,
Freneau treats American manners and events. The best of these
nonoccasional poems is, I think, "The Expedition of Timothy
Taurus, Astrologer," which Freneau notes as having been printed in
New York in the fall of 1775. The speaker in the poem is Timothy;
the occasion, his decision to take a vacation:

> My morning of life is beclouded with care!
> I will go to Passaick, I say and I swear—
> To the falls of Passaick, that elegant scene,
> Where all is so pretty, and all is so green.

Timothy goes to the resort town; and, although forced to lodge "in a
box of a house—you might call it a shed," he enjoys his holiday.
Although an astrologer, Timothy sounds more like Freneau's
pedagogue when he complains of his poor-paying profession: "For
the tinker has something that people must buy,/ While such as have
little but Latin to vend,/ On a shadow may truly be said to depend."
But Timothy forgets his piques in order to enjoy observing the
various characters gathered at the resort: a Quaker family, a deacon,
a minister, a farmer, a lawyer, a doctor, and a jockey—all with faults
and foibles that the author is quick to catch. The choice of such a
resort for locale is good; the variety of people is excusable; and their
close intercourse allows their stupidities to be revealed.

Despite the sociability of all, a few incidents indicate the ap-
proaching war. The landlady is a Tory, who "talked of the king, and
she talked of the queen,/ And she talked of her floors—that were not
very clean." In fact, she talked so much that "the Tories themselves
wished her gone to the devil." Treated in an equally light manner is
the soldier, who is used by Freneau chiefly to illustrate the admi-
ration the ladies have for a uniform: " 'O la!' cried Miss Kitty, 'how
bold he must be!/ Papa! we must beg him to join us at tea!' " But on
the second appearance of the soldier, Papa chastizes his daughter:

> "Dear Kitty," (he answered) "regard not his lace,
> The devil I see in the mould of his face:

Cockades have been famous for crazing your sex
Since Helen played truant, and left the poor Greeks."

Freneau also uses the war sentiment to mock manners in two other 1775 poems—"The Distrest Shepherdess" and "Female Frailty." In "The Distrest Shepherdess," Mariana mourns the death of Damon, who had left her to go to the siege of Quebec and had died "on the banks of the river Sorel." Although she contemplates traveling to the scene of his death, she decides to stay where she is, since "My shepherd departed I never shall meet—/ Here's Billy O'Bluster—I love him as well,/ And Damon may stay at the river Sorel." In "Female Frailty," the plot outline is essentially the same: the girl's husband has met his death in Canada, but she, consoled, promises to marry one Thyrsis, who has remained at home. "Female Frailty" has more aristocratic—and less blunt—personages than "The Distrest Shepherdess," but characters in both poems are named for pastoral rustics. Although "Female Frailty" is a more serious poem than "The Distrest Shepherdess," war is still not its major subject.

Because Freneau was an inveterate poet, one who could not think about a subject without expressing it poetically, it is inevitable that he would write poems on the current events of the time—even if he felt that such events were not worthy of a poet's notice. Thus, in the early summer of 1775, he began to describe the current events of New York City, where he had evidently settled; his earliest poem of this type is probably "The New Liberty Pole." Lines from the poem indicate that, like many New Yorkers, Freneau still believed in accommodation. His quarrel is against the laws and acts of Parliament; he is not in favor of a total break:

Though we respect the *Powers that be*,
We hold *him* an non-entity,
Who would not stir in our good cause
And rise to spurn *despotic Laws*.[24]

Most New Yorkers probably agreed with him. The delegation New York sent to the Continental Congress which met in May, 1775, was well balanced; John Jay was responsible for the "Olive Branch" petition (which the king ignored) which would have achieved the accommodation. Despite Congress's approval of this

petition, it nevertheless began to raise troops, appointed George
Washington as commander, and approved the battle for Canada.
New York, when Washington visited the city in late June, was able
to parade its troops before him. But, when the British governor of
New York, William Tryon returned to New York from a visit to
England on the same day Washington arrived to assess the military
situation, he was met and welcomed by many of the same men who
met and welcomed Washington. Tryon governed New York with the
aid of his privy council; other New Yorkers chose to be governed by
an illegally elected Provincial Congress and its committee of safety.
Thus, New Yorkers were ambivalent and served two masters.

In Freneau's political poetry of 1775, he reflected the ambiva-
lence of Whiggish New York. While "American Liberty," published
in July, contains strong anti-British, pro-provincial statements,
Freneau had returned by the end of the year to expressing hopes for
accommodation. "American Liberty," written after the battles for
Breed's and Bunker's Hills, was probably Freneau's most popular
prewar poem. As much a propaganda piece as any of Thomas Paine's
pamphlets, the poem appeals to the patriotic emotions and to the
fears and hopes of the provinces in much the same way. Freneau
begins by appealing to God to "Grant, in a cause thy wisdom must
approve,/ Undaunted valour kindled from above." The appeal is
granted: " 'Tis done, and see th'omnipotent befriends,/ The sword of
Gideon, and of God descends."

Having placed God on the provincial side, the poet justifies the
worth of the cause by tracing the history of the settlers of New
England—their departure from Popish England; their confrontation
with the trials of the new undeveloped land; the terror of their blood
being shed by the Indians. Then Freneau concludes, "Should we,
just heaven, our blood and labour spent,/ Be slaves and minions to a
parliament?" The province's cause is just; therefore, that of the
British is unjust. Freneau goes beyond attacking Parliament; he also
attacks the king (which very few did at this early date). The king has
a "vulgar soul," has not had "one gen'rous thought," and was "born
to oppress, to propagate, and rot":

> Too obstinately will'd to bow his ear
> To groaning thousands or petitions hear,
> Dare break all oaths that bind the just like fate
> Oaths, that th'Arch-Devil would blush to violate,

And, foe to truth, both oaths and honour sell,
To establish principles, the growth of hell.

Freneau's manner of character aspersion in this poem is akin to that later used by Paine, who also allied the king with the powers of Hell. Freneau also plays upon anti-Catholic fears, ones newly roused by the Quebec Act of the year before; and he considers those who support the British to be "but half reform'd and papists at the heart." Having shown the evil, Freneau shifts to the good, praises Congress ("great guardians of our freedom"), and invites the oppressed of any land to America "and bring the fiery freeborn soul along." In his conclusion, he dreams of when "the time shall come when strangers rule no more,/ Nor cruel mandates vex from Britain's shore," a time when peace shall envelop Columbia—"such is the godlike glory to be free."

But "American Liberty" is the high point of Freneau's pre-war rebellion, both in political feelings and style. It is general in that it appeals to large fears and large hopes. The rest of his poems of this period are more topical, in that they deal with local events and local personalities. Although Freneau asks in "A Political Litany" to be delivered "from Tryon the mighty, who flies from our city,/ And swelled with importance disdains the committee," he does not concentrate on the New York governor but on General Gage, the governor of Boston. The Gage poems, "General Gage's Soliloquy," "Reflections on Gage's Letter to Gen. Washington of Aug. 13," "A Voyage to Boston," and "General Gage's Confession"—all published between August and late October, 1775—use General Gage as a symbol of the British power in America. Through Freneau's attacks on Gage, the poet indicts all British as cowardly, stupid, and cruel, as rabble rousers, and as sheep-stealers. In "General Gage's Soliloquy," Gage is shown as being full of doubts about the worthiness and successfulness of his cause. He fears that the dead from Lexington and Bunker's Hill may "rise from those graves, and curse me to my face!" He can only conclude that he must look for happiness in another land.

While in the "Soliloquy" Freneau shows Gage to be representative of the British in his Hamlet-like pose of indecision and of doubt about the justice of his cause, Freneau in "Reflections on Gage's Letter" depicts him as a monster who mistreats his prisoners and who robs even the graves of his opponents in order to hang the skeletons. The poet warns the colonists: "Americans! at freedom's fane adore!/ But trust to British clemency no more." He calls them to seek their revenge: "And Carleton's Popish scull be fixt on high,/ And all like him o'er St. John's castle swing,/ To show that freedom is no trifling thing." If the poet had his way, the Americans would give the British an eye for an eye and a tooth for a tooth. "A Voyage to Boston" seems a more static poem, possibly because the form and language are derivative. In this poem, Freneau travels in imagination to Boston, is given an invisible vest by the "Genius of the River," and overhears somewhat stilted conversations in both British and provincial camps. Speakers in both camps interject references to deities such as Jove, Sol, Charon, Medusa, and Sysiphus. And the rough common soldier in the provincial camp "tho't the men, whom shining trifles sway,/ But pageant soldiers for a sun-shine day"—a thought which found more famous expression in Paine's *The Crisis*.

While Freneau uses unnaturally elaborate language in "A Voyage to Boston," and while, when appealing to Americans for firm resolve, he often refers to the example of the Romans, Freneau has in these war poems laid aside for the most part his classical and pastoral apparatus. Instead, he uses more direct description and images that are intended to shock. Even in "A Voyage to Boston," Gage is compared to Hernando Cortez, "whose faith is murder, whose religion blood," and then to a scorpion, "swoln with carnage, death, and gore." And in "American Liberty," in order to enforce his idea of the blood and labor expended by the New Englanders in order to live in a free land, Freneau includes this grisly scene of a massacre:

> Perhaps the scalp with barbarous fury torn,
> The visage mangled, and the babe unborn
> Ripp'd from its dark abode, to view the sun,
> Ere nature finish'd half she had begun.

But the poet's strongest imagery is reserved for the Tories. In "A Voyage to Boston," Freneau compares a Tory to a "Stygian hound" and asks help of a surgeon to "lay his heart and inmost entrails bare." The dissectors find inscribed on the Tory's heart, "Passive obedience to the worst of men"; and similar inscriptions appear on other parts of the body: "His crowded guts unnumber'd scrawls contain,/ The scandal of our country and the bane." Having completed his dissection, the poet reminds the reader on which side the right lies: "How like St. George, invincible I stand,/ This home bred dragon stretch'd beneath my hand!"

In these poems, the only "gentle" touches come when the poet speaks of peace. In "American Liberty," peace can only be found far away:

> Bear me, some power, as far as the winds can blow,
> As ships can travel, or as waves can flow,
> To some lone island beyond the southern pole,
> Or lands round which pacific waters roll,
> There should oblivion stop the heaving sigh,
> There should I live at least with liberty.

The only peace the poet can see for America lies in the future, but he expresses hope for a closer peace in the later poems of 1775. In "A Voyage to Boston," the American soldier wishes fervently, "God save the Congress and reform the King!" Britain may "rule our hearts again," but only if she rules as in "George the Second's reign." Freneau, like many others in late October of 1775 was still hoping for peace, but for one acquired by Britain's reformation—a vain hope.

If we accept "MacSwiggen" as being autobiographical, (dated by Freneau as being written in 1775), he seemingly sought another kind of peace. "MacSwiggen," a satire that is in spots imitative of Pope's "The Dunciad," was patched together by Freneau with bits and pieces from his satires for the Clio-Whig college battle. Who MacSwiggen is, is unknown; but we can safely assume he was a New Yorker who had the temerity to criticize Freneau's verses, and possibly his politics, although there is little mention of them in the poem. The biographical aspect of the poem appears in the first and last stanzas. In the first stanza the poet speaks of having long waited for passage to Europe, but he now changes his mind: "Why should I far in search of honour roam,/ And dunces leave to triumph here at home?" But, having described the stupidities and idiocies of MacSwiggen, the poet adopts another tack: "I to the sea with weary steps descend,/ Quit the mean conquest that such swine might yield." This poem, like some of his war poetry, ends with a description of peace:

> In distant isles some happier scene I'll choose,
> And court in softer shades the unwilling Muse,

Thrice happy there, through peaceful plains to rove,
Or the cool verdure of the orange grove,
Safe from the miscreants that my peace molest,
Miscreants, with dullness and with rage opprest.

In this instance, however, the peace is achieved because of the
absence of critics, rather than that of the British; and in peace, the
poet seeks the Muse rather than liberty. Because of the beginning
and ending, "MacSwiggen" is an uneven poem; but it is valuable
because it illustrates what may have been the poet's state of mind as
war came ever closer to New York.

When Freneau left America for his "happier scene" is unknown.
We know he was in Monmouth, New Jersey, on January 16, 1776,
where he witnessed a legal document, but his later movements are
not clear. Why Freneau left the United States just before
Washington's retreats began has always been questioned, and the
usual answer has been that his longing for peace, for quiet, for time
for poetry drove him from the land of war. According to a family
tradition, Freneau met that winter in Philadelphia a Captain Han-
son who was on his way to Santa Cruz and who invited Freneau to
accompany him. This legend implies that Freneau's decision was a
spur-of-the-moment one—perhaps little more than a desire to
experience life at sea, simple adventure. If he sought adventure,
however, he could have had it in New York City; for the Hessians
landed from Lord Howe's fleet of ships on Staten Island on July 13,
1776. Had he been a strong Tory (which his poetry indicates he was
not), he would have remained in New York and welcomed the
British. Had Freneau been a strong patriot, he would have done as
his friends did: his college-mate Brackenridge was chaplain to the
troops; Burr, a major, aided Putnam's escape from Manhattan; and
Freneau's cousin John Morin Scott headed the New York troops.

Above all, Freneau left his widowed mother, his sisters, and his
brothers at home in a New Jersey which was thought to be the next
objective of the British. It would have taken a very strong desire for
peace to be able to say "a plague on both your houses," when, at
twenty-three, he was his mother's eldest son. But he did leave, first
for Santa Cruz, then for the British-held Bermudas; and he did not
return for two years. He left not as an established poet but as one
who had experimented widely with ideas as well as verse styles. He
had written poems of manners and morals, poems about contem-

porary events and about ancient ones, poems of melancholy and of satire, poems arousing patriotism and action, and poems celebrating quiet retreats. He was already a man who could no more resist writing poetry on any event or idea that he came across than he could voluntarily stop breathing.

CHAPTER 2

Occasional Poetry

FRENEAU, always an occasional poet, recorded in verse any
event that caught his attention. The most famous of Freneau's
occasional poems were written between the years 1776 and 1790,
and they describe the people and places of his initial wanderings and
also his reaction to current events when he returned to America
during the Revolution. His second period of occasional verse was
that of his last voyages and the War of 1812. The contrasts between
the poems about the events of the Revolutionary War and those
about the War of 1812 are interesting, as are the contrasts between
his first look at foreign customs and his last. But even more interesting are the poems about everyday events, for Freneau's
characteristics are displayed most clearly in them: his eager interest
in the unusual, his quick rage at the least injustice, and his perception of the incongruous. These occasional poems show Freneau to
be a man easily fascinated—and a fascinating man.

I *Collections of Poetry*

Freneau's early occasional verse was published in the 1786 *Poems
of Philip Freneau* and in the 1788 *The Miscellaneous Works of Mr.
Philip Freneau*, and his later war poetry was published in *A Collection of Poems on American Affairs* in 1815. The 1786 volume is
dominated by occasional verse, and the poems appear in the volume
in approximate chronological order: his college poems first, then the
poems written against the British in New York, the verse written in
the West Indies, and then the mass of poems about the Revolution
from his Philadelphia years. These occasional poems are interspersed with a rare philosophical or Romantic poem, such as "On
a Lady's Singing Bird," "The Dying Indian," or "The Seasons
Moralized." The "Foe to Tyrant" poems are included as a group,
and the various New Year's verses written by Freneau are clustered

46

at the close of the volume. For the most part, this collection would have its greatest appeal at a time close to the events which the poems chronicle.

Freneau's change of life-style is reflected in the 1788 *Miscellaneous Works*. No longer a newspaperman who was abreast of all the current events, Freneau was now a trader on the East coast. His interests were no longer national affairs but local and personal ones. This volume, which consists of intermixed poetry and prose, contains essays, previously contributed to the *Freeman's Journal*, which are descriptive of current conditions of society but which do not deal very much with current events. While the poems reflect to a certain extent Freneau's reaction to personal events, few are concerned with national events, a great contrast with the poetry of the 1786 volume. The 1788 poems are new ones—that is, none published in the 1786 edition—although some stem from his pre-West Indian years, as do "The Pictures of Columbus" and perhaps "The Hermit of Saba." Again, unlike the 1786 edition, the poetry in *Miscellaneous Works* exhibits a broad range of poetic styles and a variety of subject matter. In this respect, the 1815 edition resembles the *Miscellaneous Works*—the war poems are interspersed with poetry about more universal themes. All of his published volumes show Freneau letting his poetry express all aspects of his character and interests.

II *West Indian Interlude—Early Poetry Recording Voyages*

. Despite the national and international turmoil of the Revolutionary years, Freneau found in the West Indies a special place that he could transform into his poetic Eden. His poems written there show that the lush beauty and the warmth of the islands must have deeply impressed the young man from New Jersey, and their remoteness from the colonial struggles made an even deeper impression. Freneau's attitude toward the natural endowments of the islands may be all that a Romantic may ask; but, as soon as he begins to talk about the islands' inhabitants, he becomes once more the close observer of the follies of man. The travel poems, early and late, while recording his findings about the geography and society of strange lands, do more: in their emphasis and selection of detail, they reflect Freneau's values.

Freneau had ample opportunity to visit many of the Atlantic and Caribbean islands during the early years. From 1776 to 1778, he

sailed with a trader to Bermuda and to the various islands surrounding Santa Cruz, the home base; and we know from one of his
poems that he probably also touched at Jamaica. Later, after his
return to the States, he traded with St. Eustacia and Jamaica again;
and during his last series of voyages after 1800, he traveled as far as
Madeira. On his first trips, however, he was fortunate enough to be
associated with a native of Santa Cruz who could impart to him the
local lore and who could introduce him to the various island
societies and customs. He was able to see the colonial systems at
work—Santa Cruz was Danish; St. Eustacia, Dutch; Bermuda and
Jamaica, British; and Freneau probably also touched at French and
Spanish islands. The first trip to the West Indies, then, was valuable
for his later career as ship's captain and trader. Poetically, the trip
gave him an ideal against which to view and contrast contemporary
events and circumstances.

Freneau's favorite island was Santa Cruz. In a letter printed in the
United States Magazine in 1779, he compares the island to Paradise,
a comparison which often marks his poetry of the West Indies:
"even those who have no taste to admire the beauties of nature,
would at the view be forced to confess that the vales of Paradise
were now displayed to the eye in their primaeval beauty."[1]But
Freneau continues the analogy; Santa Cruz may be Paradise, but
the world is populated with fallen men who war with one another:
"My agreeable residence at this place for above two years off and on
during the wars in America, renders the idea of it but too pleasing,
and makes me feel much the same anxiety at a distance from it as
Adam did after he was banished from the bowers of Eden."[2]

The beauties of Santa Cruz became even more beautiful as
Freneau contrasted them with the horrors of war. While the letter
to the *United States Magazine* gives a traveler's account of Santa
Cruz, the poem, "The Beauties of Santa Cruz," which follows the
letter, has as persona a defiant peace-lover who is unwilling to
budge from his haven. Although Freneau greatly revised the poem
and enlarged it (swelling it from 52 to 108 stanzas), the organization
and the intent of the first, 1779, version were not altered—in fact,
the first printing may be a more unified poem than the later revised
one.

"The Beauties of Santa Cruz," justly Freneau's most famous West
Indian poem, is ostensibly addressed to a "northern swain" and
proposes that he leave his bleak winters and enjoy the sun. Fre-

neau, in the opening lines, makes much of the contrast between heat and cold, between the ice of the North and the beauties of Santa Cruz: "In happiest climate lies this envied isle,/ Trees bloom throughout the year, streams ever flow,/ And fragrant Flora wears a lasting smile." Even the ocean around the isle is calm, and colorful fish please the eye.

In the 1779 version, Freneau devotes the next section of the poem to a catalog of the flora of the island. He describes the mangrove, orange, lime, lemon, plum, cashew, papaw, "plantane"; but he gives special honors to the coconut and sugar cane: "Hence comes the planter's wealth, hence commerce sends/ Such floating piles to traverse half the main." Only occasionally during this cataloging does he stray from his adulation. In describing the manchineel, Freneau warns, "O shun the dangerous tree, nor taste, like Eve,/ This interdicted fruit in Eden's ground." And, in describing the shade offered by the luxuriant growth along a stream, he becomes melancholy about the Indians who once enjoyed the spot: "The lovers fled, the tearful stream remains,/ And only I console it with my lay." In the next section, as if compelled by reason to present a complete picture, Freneau shows the faults of this Eden. There are occasional hurricanes, and the "Ethiopian swain" is wretched: "He pants a land of freedom and repose,/ Where cruel slavery never sought to reign."

Santa Cruz is so lovely, the poet wonders how he could ever leave:

> Fain would I view my native climes again,
> But murder marks the cruel Briton there—
> Contented here I rest, in spite of pain,
> And quaff the enlivening juice in spite of care.

In the next few stanzas, Freneau once again correlates winter with gloom, summer with cheeriness of mind; and he once again invites his friend to come to the sun: "Then shepherd haste, and leave behind thee far/ The bloody plains and iron glooms above." If, however, the shepherd still loves his own land, Freneau tells him to "repell the tyrant who thy peace invades,/ While, pleas'd, I trace the vales of Santa Cruz,/ And sing with rapture her inspiring shades." The poem seems almost a verse letter to a friend; and, because the poem fits the events of Freneau's life during this period

so well, it is difficult to refrain from reading it as picturing his true
state of mind.

But the poem is also interesting for its inclusion of themes and
images found in most of Freneau's West Indian poetry. In "Santa
Cruz," he refers to the land as an Eden; but the Eden he has found
includes elements of its own destruction, and he does not quite trust
the Eden's stability. The immediate metaphorical threat is the
manchineel, but other lines indicate Freneau's wariness. The sugar
cane, which is praised, is nevertheless compared to the lotus, and
the eaters, to Ulysses and his men: "Taste not the enchanting
plant—to taste forbear,/ If ever thou wouldst reach thy much lov'd
home." As in the *Odyssey*, there is the feeling that the Lotus Eaters
somehow do wrong. Other ills in the garden, slightly indicated here
but emphasized in other poems, are the institution of slavery and
man's avarice.

"The Beauties of Santa Cruz" shows the poet's vacillation between war and peace, between the concept of man in paradise and
man removed from it. He also shifts between the interests of the
Enlightenment and the interests of the pre-Romantics. In his concern for listing exact names and properties of the native plants, he
shows the interests of Linnaeus, shared by many men in the new
world, including Thomas Jefferson. His attention to detail as he
describes how things work also marks the neoclassic man, as in this
description of making flour:

> Cassada shrubs abound, whose poison root,
> Supplies the want of snow-white Northern flour;
> This grated fine, and steep'd in water fair,
> Forsakes each particle of noxious power.

But the melancholy derived from the passing of the Indians and the
poet's sympathy with the weeping stream are characteristic of the
pre-Romantics. This combination in Freneau of his scientific
curiosity and his projecting spirit, with his attitude that Nature,
without man's interference, is best, is also illustrated in his prose
account of the island of St. James: "Were a gentleman of fortune and
taste to purchase the spot, he might make it by the assistance of art,
a most enchanting residence. Tho' as to my own part the rude
irregularity of nature pleases me more than the completest strokes
of art." But Freneau also adds his strain of traditional morality:

"There is soil enough to contain his bones, and even the largest continent when he is dead can give him no more."[3]

In other poems of observation of the West Indies, Freneau intensifies the theme that unspoiled nature is preferable to man and his works. In "Lines Written at Port-Royal," the poet, after describing the location of the famous old town, concludes with a farewell to "fair Kingston's plain;/ Where Nature still the toils of art transcends." The theme is repeated in "Stanzas Written at the foot of Monte Souffriere": "These Indian isles . . ./ Art hardly told us where they lay,/ 'Till tyranny their charms defaced." All is summarized in the line, "Man frowns—and only nature smiles."

In "The Hermit of Saba," an early poem, Freneau again mourns the passing of innocence with the arrival of Europeans. In this poem, a dialogue between three mariners and a hermit, the mariners kill the hermit for his treasure, which they imagine to be gold, but which the hermit considered to be peace. The third mariner, in remorse, imagines the shade of the hermit following him, saying: "Perdition on these fiends from Europe,/ Whose bloody malice, or whose thirst for gold,/ Fresh from the slaughter-house of innocence/ Unpeoples isles, and lays the world in ruin!" The golden age of the islands lies in the past, a time when the lands were untouched by the European. These poems give little hope that man might eventually be able to construct another golden age.

But Freneau's poems based on observation of the lands he visited contain more than philosophical generalizations about the state of man. He also describes the manners and attitudes of man in society, seizing specific occasions to describe man's folly. In "The Jamaica Funeral," he presents a series of pictures of the funeral of a great man—one who is not mourned sincerely by any of the funeral guests. Several characters are pictured, including the widow who dances after the rites are over; but the central butt of Freneau's sharp scorn is the priest who cares more about the present life—especially its wine—than about the future one or about his duty to prepare his parishioners for it. On another occasion, when he was refused water by a British official in Jamaica, Freneau composed "To the Keeper of the King's Water Works," in which he not only satirizes the king, his government, and red tape but also asks the keeper to tell the king "that Nature is no miser here;/ Tell him—that he withholds—what beggars give." In these two poems, Freneau chronicles faults that could be found in man everywhere but that happen to have been observed in the West Indies.

Freneau's greatest displeasure with the West Indies was provoked by the institution of slavery. Sometimes, as in "Lines Written at Port-Royal," his feelings take the form of pity for the slaves' lack of freedom: the Negro "casts his view beyond the adjacent strand/ And points, still grieving, to his native land." A more powerful description is in "To Sir Toby," which is sometimes titled "The Island Field Hand," in which Freneau describes the cruelties of the overseers, the whips, the gibbets, the iron collars, and the lack of food. He then admits this blot on nature's beauties:

> Talk not of blossoms, and your endless spring;
> What joy, what smile, can scenes of misery bring?—
> Though Nature, here, has every blessing spread,
> Poor is the labourer—and how meanly fed!

Although Freneau admits that the presence of man has destroyed Eden, he never quite abandoned his dream of finding peace and contentment on some quiet, uninhabited island.

III   *Later Poetry of Travels*

Freneau was proud of being a seafarer and ship's captain. In a letter written during his post–Revolutionary War voyages, his pride in this occupation, an unusual one for a man of letters, is evident: "Read all history, ransack libraries, call tradition to your aid, search all records, examine a million of manuscripts on vellum, on parchment, on paper, on marble, on what you please, and I defy you to find the most distant hint, of any *poet,* in any age or country, from Hesiod down to Peter Pindar having been *trusted* with the controul or possession of any thing fit to be mentioned or compared with this same barque, which, you say, *I have the misfortune to command.*"[4] As both poet and ship's master, Freneau wrote not only of lands visited but also of events encountered at sea. The occasion did not have to be a major one for him to compose a poem on it.

"On the Crew of a Certain Vessel" is spun from his observation of the similarity between names of the crewmen and celebrated clergymen: "A graceless Sherlock trims the sails,/ And Bunyan heaves the log." But Freneau often had more than the crew for his companionship; he carried passengers as well as cargo. Although two of his passengers were lost overboard during a gale in 1788, a safer voyage was destined for the young Quaker lady whom Freneau hoped to immortalize in his poem "To Lydia." Although the young lady was fearful, she lightened the journey for the captain:

> Delighted with a face so fair,
> I half forgot my weight of care
> The dangerous shoal, that seaward runs,
> Encircled moons, and shrouded suns.

The poem illustrates well Freneau's dual role of poet and seaman because it expresses his appreciation of beauty and also his seaman's responsibilities.

But responsibilities had always to come first; he could not be negligent and survive. "Verses, Made at Sea, in a Heavy Gale" is a carefully constructed response to a dangerous occasion. Written by Freneau after experiencing a hurricane off Jamaica in 1784, the poem establishes the contrast between those who are safe and those who are unsafe. Land dwellers have recourse to shelter; sea rovers, none. The last three stanzas, after supposing a physical lack of safety on the part of the sailors, somewhat obscurely suggest also a metaphysical lack of safety. The sailors, because of the storm, might be "buried low, by far too deep,/ On coral beds, unpitied, sleep!" The fourth stanza then begins, "but what a strange, uncoasted strand/ Is that, where fate permits no day—/ No charts have we to mark that land,/ No compass to direct that way." But the fifth stanza seems to return to the actual physical surroundings: "What comfort on this raging sea?" The ship no longer responds to the pilot: "Alone she gropes her trackless way,/ While mountains burst on either side—/ Thus, skill and science both must fall;/ And ruin is the lot of all." We are tempted to read the last line as applying to both the physical and metaphysical situations of the poem, but we do so with no assurance. Read only on the physical level, the concluding stanza is grim enough to portray the helplessness of men when faced with a hurricane.

The greatest differences between the poems of the first voyages and those of the last are in tone and voice. The poems of the voyages undertaken after 1800 are still travelogues that record Freneau's visits to the various ports of call. But these poems have a more relaxed persona, one who expresses only a perfunctory desire to remain in the tropical lands. Freneau utilizes the persona of a sailor who enjoys the lands he visits but who must return to his business, leaving only a poem behind him. The earlier travel poems contain Freneau's ravings over natural beauties or reveal his scorn for the institution of slavery. But these later poems have a more tolerant speaker, one more mature and wiser in the ways of the world, and, although they lack Freneau's earlier exuberance, they are more polished than the earlier ones.

Although these later poems show a Freneau who judges less harshly of men and their ways, some are still didactic, as is "Answer to a Card of Invitation To Visit a Nunnery at Garrichica, on the North Side of Teneriffe" (1804). This poem is built on contrasts between those who stay and those who go, those who live secluded from the world, and those who face its dangers. The speaker first declines with regret the invitation to visit the nunnery. His sponsor can "stay and sip Canary wines" and "talk, familiar with the nuns," but he has "many a weary mile to go" and can "think no more of Teneriffe." When Freneau elaborates on these basic facts, the nunnery is described as a remote garden of fruit, but the fruit is forbidden; the nuns are guarded by "jealous priests." As contrast to the nuns, Freneau offers "our western fair" who "go where they please, do what they will." Once more the poet declines the invitation: "Should I attempt the nuns to accost/ The priests might growl, and all be lost." His duty lies in braving "the lee-ward shore, the rocky shoal," with Neptune threatening at every moment to gulp his cargo of wine. Nevertheless, he prefers these dangers: "But here's a health to Neptune's sons/ Who man the yard—nor dream of nuns." Although Freneau obviously disapproves of nunneries, he expresses disapproval fancifully in keeping with the tone of a letter written to entertain a friend. Freneau has seized on a very minor occasion to create a poem.

Indeed, the slightest of occasions gave Freneau the impulse to create some of his most urbane poems. "On Seniora Julia" captures in its lines a young belle who is vivacious at a party until her fancy, "Almagro," leaves to hear the latest news from France, whereupon she "feign'd an aching head" and went to bed. The subject is slight, but the amusement and good humor with which the speaker views Julia's change of spirits makes the poem worth while. A more serious incident is treated in "The Nautical Rendezvous Written at a house in Guadaloupe, in 1800, where they were collecting Recruits for a Privateer." Freneau expresses wonder that these recruits would roam "in a moving jail," that they "prefer a boisterous, mad career,/ A broken leg, and wounds severe,/ To all the joys that can be found/ On mountain top or furrow'd ground." But the speaker finally sees the reason: there must be such people "who will support through every blast,/ The shatter'd ship, the falling mast" in order to defend France from her enemies and to support "the sacred cause of liberty." While this poem treats a subject dear to Freneau, the cause of France, he treats it lightly and urbanely.

Most of these later travel poems concentrate on describing people rather than the lands they inhabit. In these poems, the personality of the speaker dominates; before, the marvels being described had done so. Although "Stanzas Written at the Island of Madeira" has a more muted speaker, the force of geniality and the play of fancy present in this poem do not occur in earlier verses. In fact, these elements prevent the reader from feeling the horror of the situation—a horror conveyed by the prose introduction to the poem: "On the fatal and unprecedented torrents of water which collected from the mountains on the ninth of October, 1803, and destroyed a considerable part of the city of Funchal, drowned a vast number of people, and damaged, to a great amount, several plantations and villages in that neighborhood." By its casualness, the first stanza establishes the tone of the poem:

> The rude attack, if none will tell,
> On Bacchus, in his favorite isle;
> If none in verse describe it well,
> If none assume a poet's style
> These devastations to display;—
> Attend me, and perhaps I may.

Freneau not only describes the human losses, such as a son, torn from his mother's arms, and describes churches and bridges destroyed but also depicts the "cheery god" who "sought his caves in wild dismay/ And left the heavens to have their way." The best passages in the poem describe, with Miltonesque phrasing, the effect of the storm on the landscape:

> From heights immense, with force unknown,
> Enormous rocks and mangled trees
> Were headlong hurl'd and hurrying down,

> Fix'd their foundation in the seas!
> Or, rushing with a mountain's weight,
> Hurl'd to the deeps their domes of state.

The sailor will long note the flood's effects on the harbor; but, Freneau concludes, "these ravages may time repair,/ But he and I will not be there."

Freneau again has created the persona of the visitor who comes, records, leaves, and dedicates his poems to his friends of the port as mementos of his visits. Freneau makes no such skillful use of persona in his earlier poems. In the prewar travel poems he adopts, essentially, only two poses: that of the appreciative poet and lover of beauty and that of the angry young man who is impatient about the vices of men. This latter pose he retained, to the exclusion of almost every other attitude, in his poems written after he returned from his West Indian idyll to the scenes of the American Revolution.

IV Poems about the Revolution

For some reason, Freneau left his haven of peace in the spring of 1778; and, after a six-week stay in Bermuda, he returned to New Jersey on July 9. Less than a week later, he enlisted in the New Jersey Militia and stayed on its rolls for two years. During his two-year term, Freneau continued his career at sea by serving on trading ships and possibly on a privateer. Despite his naval activity, he found time to contribute extensively to Brackenridge's *United States Magazine* in 1779. In 1780, Freneau's most publicized war experience took place when he was imprisoned on a British naval hulk in New York harbor. Released after a short imprisonment, Freneau composed his most famous war poem, "The British Prison Ship," which was printed in 1781. Freneau's poetic production increased greatly after his imprisonment, but chiefly, I think, because he was associated closely (he may have been editor) with the Philadelphia *Freeman's Journal* from 1781 to 1783.

As was usual with Freneau, however, he did not limit himself to one occupation. While working for the newspaper, he also served as clerk to Ebenezer Hazard, the Continental postmaster; and he also translated French articles and books for American publication, most notably Abbé Claude Robin's *New Travels through North America*, which appeared in July, 1783. Since Freneau now seemed to have abandoned all thought of returning to Santa Cruz, Philadelphia was an ideal place to be for the composition of verse on current events. As the seat of Congress, all news traveled there; all decisions were made there; and, we suspect, many rumors were started there. In addition to the business of the war, Philadelphia was naturally an active city—it was the center of shipping and trading, as well as the publishing center of the colonies.

The British center for trade, publishing, and propaganda was New York City. Since 1775, a steady decline in the amount and quality of propaganda put forth by the Whigs had occurred, but the British and Tory propaganda had increased. The British dominated the press, chiefly through James Rivington's *Royal Gazette* in New York. In it, the propagandists conjured the specter of a French takeover of all the backcountry lands, and the French imposition of popery on America. Congress, the paper's readers were told, was composed of no one but low-born rogues who were bankrupting the country with their financial schemes; they were also told that the officers of high rank in the Continental Army were against the war, a theme increasingly mentioned after the Arnold affair.

Since the number of presses in America had decreased during the war, there were many Whig readers of this propaganda. Richard Henry Lee, in 1781, writing of the approach of Cornwallis, complained that "the enemies design seems to be by great distress and much delusion to bring over the minds of the people—it must be confessed that they have the fairest opportunity, for we have no press in the country."[5] It is no wonder, then, that much of Freneau's occasional verse of this time was aimed at discrediting not only the Tory printers and their claims but also all key British figures.

A long tradition has existed that Freneau wrote his war poetry only out of a sense of duty, and such a view has been expressed by H. H. Clark: "Poet of war he was, but only through patriotic compunction; his heart naturally yearned toward gentler themes of fancy and imagination; the great bulk of his writing is undeniably imperfect, crude, and often bitter, but this does not represent the real Freneau,—rather the ardent poet who has lent his pen to a cause which his finer nature abhors."[6] But this view concentrates only on one side of Freneau and neglects the other that enjoyed satirizing man's follies. It also fails to account for the obvious gusto of

his college satires and for the fact that Freneau rarely resisted a good
literary fight, be it with the British in two wars or with a now-
obscure literary critic. Then, too, Freneau was not slow to record
the war: he returned to New Jersey in July, and he published that
fall "America Independent," a lengthy poem, dedicated to the
propaganda battle.

"America Independent" attacks the institution of monarchy, first
generally (*"Kings are the choicest curse that man e'er knew!"*), then
specifically with a personal attack on King George:

> In him we see the depths of baseness joined,
> Whate'er disgraced the dregs of human kind;
> Cain, Nimrod, Nero—fiends in human guise,
> Herod, Domitian—these in judgment rise,
> And, envious of his deeds, I hear them say
> None but a George could be more vile than they.

As in his college verse, Freneau freely sprinkles historical allusions
and freely wages as before the *ad hominem* argument in his poem.
In "America Independent," although Burgoyne shares with George
the blows of the poet, Freneau devotes the best (although not the
most beautiful) part of the composition to the Tories. Few of
Freneau's passages are as Gothic as this one that describes the
Tories:

> So vile a crew the world ne'er saw before,
> And grant, ye pitying heavens, it may no more:
> If ghosts from hell infest our poisoned air,
> Those ghosts have entered their base bodies here;
> Murder and blood is still their dear delight—
> Scream round their roofs, ye ravens of the night!
> Whene'er they wed, may demons and despair,
> And grief and woe, and blackest night be there;
> Fiends leagued from hell the nuptial lamp display,
> Swift to perdition light them on their way,
> Round the wide world their devilish squadrons chace,
> To find no realm, that grants one resting place.

Freneau pleads the greatly changed condition of his country that he
found upon his return as the reason for his anger and disgust. He
advises his countrymen "no dull debates, or tedious counsels know,/
But rush at once, embodied, on your foe." "America Independent"

is a good example of war propaganda: it ridicules the enemy, traces the present miseries of the people, describes the glorious future when the battle will be won, and concludes with a call for greater effort. Few of Freneau's poems contain all of these elements, but his first war poem after his return did so.

Freneau soon followed "America Independent" with a series of poems mocking the morals and abilities of key British figures. Two of these poems are similar in that they attack the weakness and vacillation of King George while associating him with Hell's cause. "George the Third's Soliloquy" shows the king tortured by dreams and omens of ill-fortune. His conclusion that, when he began the wars, "the fiends of darkness then possessed my mind" is a theme expanded in "A Dialogue Between His Britannic Majesty and Mr. Fox." Freneau has King George compare Lord North's promises of victory to Satan's tempting of Judas—"these have allur'd me to the jaws of hell."

A poem combining religious and Gothic imagery is "The Loyalists," one of Freneau's most powerful war poems. Once more the Gothic element is dominant as he talks of the Tories, whom he compares to wolves, bloodhounds, and devils. Then, as if asking forgiveness for his roughness, Freneau explains that once, indeed, his muse "sung the pleasures of the plantain shade," but was forced to change her topic:

> But when she saw your blazing turrets fall,
> Your slaughter'd friends in vain for mercy call,
> Your captive sons with British poison die,
> Your fields laid waste and total conquest nigh;
> Griev'd at the view she rais'd a bolder strain,
> Expos'd the tyrant and deny'd his reign.

Though all looks black for the rebels' cause, Freneau reassures his readers that their triumph is inevitable; heaven is on their side: "Long do the skies their righteous rage suspend,/ That hotter vengeance may from thence descend."[7] Although "The Loyalists" was never reprinted after its appearance in Brackenridge's magazine in July, a great many of its lines were later incorporated by Freneau into "The British Prison Ship."

For his villains, Freneau uses Gothic and biblical imagery; for his heroes, he is more apt to use classical imagery. "On the New

American Frigate Alliance" consists of a discussion between Neptune and Triton who are admiring a new ship sailing the seas. The ship, announces Triton, is the *Alliance;* and her duty is to guard the coasts instead of selfishly sailing the more lucrative waters of the West Indies. A new argonaut, the *Alliance* sails to attain neither wealth nor adventure but to vanquish tyranny. The *Alliance,* however, met the fate of most of the other American navy frigates; on sea or on land there was little good news. But Freneau sought to appeal to the pride of the rebels by describing in inflated terms one loss in "On the Death of Captain Nicholas Biddle":

> Say, who commands that dismal blaze,
> Where yonder starry streamer plays?
> Does Mars with Jove engage!
> 'Tis Biddle wings those angry fires,
> Biddle, whose bosom Jove inspires,
> With more than mortal rage.

Despite Jove, Biddle, a really talented captain, lost his ship and his life.

In 1781, Freneau took advantage of a personal encounter with the British and of the colonial outrage at British prison conditions to publish his most successful war poem, "The British Prison Ship." En route to the West Indies, Freneau's ship was captured; and he was imprisoned. In a short note to his West Indian host, Freneau wittily relates the bare facts: "I take this opportunity to inform you that instead of arriving as I fondly promised myself at the fragrant groves and delectable Plains of Santa Cruz, to enjoy the fruits and flowers of that happy clime, I was unfortunately taken and confined on board a Prison Ship at New York, and afterwards in a Hospital ship where the damnable draughts of a German doctor afforded far different feelings to my Stomach than the juice of the Orange or more nourishing milk of the cocoa."[8]

Although Freneau adopts in this note a light tone (fortunately, his imprisonment was not long), other accounts of the prison ships were horrifying. In 1778, an account of the suffering of the men in the New York prison ships was written by a man who had just escaped from one and was printed in the *Connecticut Gazette:* "Their sickly countenances and ghastly looks were truly horrible, some swearing and blaspheming, some crying, praying and wringing their hands and stalking about like ghosts, others delirious, raving and storming;

some groaning and dying, all panting for breath; some dead and corrupting, air so foul at times that a lamp could not be kept burning, by reason of which the boys were not missed till they had been dead ten days."[9] The prison ships had long been notorious among the Americans; indeed, American naval commanders had used the ships as arguments to persuade their sailors to fight on rather than surrender to the enemy, and newspapers had used accounts like the one above for effective propaganda.

If only because of its length and its form, Freneau's "The British Prison Ship" rises above sheer propaganda. Freneau, who expended great care on this poem, transforms a personal experience into an almost epic one. The poem, divided into three cantos, uses much of the machinery of the epic poem. The poet appeals to Clio for inspiration, alludes to a variety of gods, and attributes to the boatswain the traditional prayer to the heavens for aid in the upcoming battle. But, at the same time, Freneau uses nautical terms that did not meet the neoclassic demands that the vocabulary be elevated yet comprehensible to the audience. Written in couplets, the poem is vigorous and forceful, extremely unified and well-constructed. It is good poetry while being effective propaganda.

In canto I, Freneau describes the building of the ship *Aurora* and her putting to sea. The enemy is sighted, the *Aurora* flees toward the shore, and the boatswain voices his prayer: " 'And now, to sum up every curse in one,/ May latent flames, to save us, intervene,/ And hell-ward drive them from their magazine!' " But the *Aurora* is becalmed, the *Iris* approaches, and the two ships fire:

> Another blast, as fatal in its aim,
> Wing'd by destruction, through our rigging came,
> And, whistling tunes from hell upon its way,
> Shrouds, stays, and braces tore at once away,
> Sails, blocks, and oars in scatter'd fragments fly—
> Their softest language was—*submit, or die!*

The *Aurora* surrenders, and the prisoners are conveyed to New York only to find "that Death was better than the prisoner's fate." A comparison between canto I and the earlier poem of naval defeat, "On the Death of Captain Biddle," shows how "The British Prison Ship" departs from the usual. Both poems use the neoclassic machinery, but the realistic detail used in "The British Prison Ship" makes this battle more real and immediate.

Canto II begins with generalities and with a diatribe against the Tories, borrowed from "The Loyalists." Freneau then names the prison ship, the *Scorpion*, and some of the miseries endured—work at the pumps, exposure to sun, and lack of food and fresh water. At night, all are driven below to sleep where they can; next morning, "the dead were past their pain, the living groan." The guards are nothing but petty tyrants who take pleasure in inflicting pain. They are British, Irish, Hessian; but the worst are the Tories: by them, America has been "stung by the serpents whom ourselves had nurs'd." Given the conditions aboard ship, illness was inevitable:

> Hunger and thirst to work our woe combine,
> And mouldy bread, and flesh of rotten swine,
> The mangled carcase, and the batter'd brain,
> The doctor's poison, and the captain's cane,
> The soldier's musquet, and the steward's debt,
> The evening shackle, and the noon-day threat.

Such a catalog, in couplets, is an achievement.

Canto III relates the transfer of the speaker to the hospital ship *Hunter*, where "Death strode stately, while the victims groan'd." In this canto, three portraits are given—those of the doctor, the Chief of Physicians, and the captain. These portraits are heavily satirical; and, although the verse is weaker than that of the rest of the poem, some of the couplets are well-pointed. The longest portrait is that of the Hessian doctor: "here uncontroul'd he exercis'd his trade,/ And grew experienced by the deaths he made." The Chief of Physicians, who visited the ship once, was armed with a scowl and two pistols: "that, by the gods!—with such a load of steel/ He came, we thought, to murder, not to heal." The captain vented his spleen on the prisoners: "he swore, till every prisoner stood aghast,/ And thought him Satan in a brimstone blast."

When the inevitable deaths begin, the prisoners are forced to bury the dead in shallow graves of sand. Freneau allows the pathetic sentiment to dominate only briefly, for he concludes the poem with a call to arms and with a thorough condemnation of the British. He asks the Americans to "glut revenge on this detested foe":

> Can you forget the greedy Briton's ire,
> Your fields in ruin, and your domes on fire,
> No age, no sex from lust and murder free,

> And, black as night, the hell born refugee!
> Must York forever your best blood entomb,
> And these gorg'd monsters triumph in their doom.

Thomas Paine could hardly have issued such a resounding call. No quarter is to be given the British: "Rouse from your sleep, and crush the thievish band,/ Defeat, destroy, and sweep them from the land." Once more, as in "America Independent," in this last section of canto III, Freneau has created rousing patriotic verse. The poem, as a whole, lacks subtlety, for Freneau relies overmuch on name-calling to convince. Nonetheless, this fault is balanced by the large number of concrete, graphic details of the conditions endured.

His prison experience over and recorded, Freneau spent the fall in New Jersey, but his association soon began with the *Freeman's Journal* to which he contributed the largest portion of his Revolutionary War verse. In his patriotic verse of this period, Freneau most often devotes his rhymes to discrediting the British, to vilifying the Tories, and to ridiculing the Tory printers. Only very late in the war did Freneau have opportunity to record occasions of American victories, and such victories must have seemed a long way off in the summer and fall of 1780. There were no triumphs, no decisive battles, no end in sight to the frustrating *status quo*. Morale was low, chiefly because of the recent revelation of Benedict Arnold's treachery; and it was made more fearful by James Rivington's reports in his *Royal Gazette* that other American officers shared Arnold's sentiments. Consequently, Freneau spent part of his recuperation from imprisonment dealing with Arnold's story in a work, left incomplete and never published, that was in a form new to Freneau—a verse and prose drama entitled "The Spy." Unlike Freneau's other works that record the war, the form is more Shakespearean than neoclassic: it is written in blank verse, rather than couplets; there is no unity of place, the scene shifts from West Point to New York to a remote inn; comic characters are included, a subplot involving Andre and his Lucinda is present; Arnold is given several soliloquies; and songs are interspersed generously throughout the action.

Arnold's motivation, according to Freneau, is easily read—avarice rules his soul. John André declares this fact to Sir Henry Clinton as the two first plan the taking of West Point, and the same thesis is repeated by Freneau at the close after the plot has been discovered.

But Arnold, as pictured in "The Spy," is not completely villainous,
since Freneau endows him with a conscience to battle with, as in his
first soliloquy, where Arnold shows irresolution:

> But art thou, Arnold, less than murderer,
> Who thus prepare to stab thy bleeding country?
> And can I then descend to be a traitor!
> By honest toils a name have I acquired,
> Great and unequalled in the rolls of fame.

Nevertheless, Arnold achieves justification for his anticipated deed:
"The people are not dull republicans,/ By nature they incline to
monarchy." In his second soliloquy, just before his meeting with
André, Arnold still feels his conscience; he asks for darkness to cover
his deed: "Peace to this gloomy grove that sees me acting/ What
open daylight would disdain to own." But, Freneau did not publish
this portrait of Arnold—in his published poems of Arnold, he allows
no such picture of the doubts that must have beset the defector; and
the reader is forbidden any sympathy for him. In "The 10th Ode
Horace's Book of Epodes Imitated," composed to celebrate Arnold's
departure from New York, the poet's wish is that his ship will be
attacked by every force of nature, "may not one friendly star that
night be seen."

To Freneau, Tories were also traitors; but his verse dealing with
them is so much lighter that it seems that he enjoyed mocking their
situation. To Freneau, the typical Tory was an opportunist who had
unfortunately bet on the wrong side. A series of poems, supposedly
written by a New York Tory, summarize their story, and Freneau's
treatment of it. The first, "A New-York Tory to His Friend in
Philadelphia," published in the fall of 1781, represents the New
York writer as full of concern for his friend who remained behind the
American lines: "when our armies, victorious, shall clear that vile
nest/ You may chance, though a Tory, to swing with the rest." After
recounting the desperate plight of the rebel army and navy, the
writer concludes that "the rebellion is done."

This first poem reflects the grim situation of the rebels; but, by
the summer of 1782, the situation had changed. "On General
Robertson's Proclamation" has the Tories protesting British militia
duty; and, according to Freneau, they resolve "come let us turn
round and rebelliously sing,/ Huzza for the Congress!—the de'il

take the king." By May, 1783, with the publication of "A New-York Tory's Epistle," Freneau is somewhat sympathetic; the sharpest bite comes when the New Yorker congratulates his Philadelphia friend on having hidden his Toryism, thereby escaping expulsion. The New Yorker ruefully draws the moral: "Henceforth must I, abandon'd and distrest,/ Knock at the door of pride, a beggar guest,/ And learn from years of misery and pain/ Not to oppose fair Freedom's cause again!" In "A New York Tory's Epistle," published in 1785, Freneau voices once more the complaints of the Tory. He has the Tory ask for forgiveness for he wants to return from Nova Scotia. These Tory poems, light and mocking, are far different from the earlier, heavy-handed, name-calling attacks on the enemy.

While Freneau was somewhat sympathetic toward the Tories, such sympathy was not shown to a specific Tory, James Rivington, the editor of the *Royal Gazette*. The Rivington poems, which appeared in the *Freeman's Journal* from February, 1782, to December, 1783, form a well-unified satiric attack on the printer. The dominant theme, emphasized in each poem, is that Rivington is skilled in lies and that his confederate, friend, and master is Satan. Freneau obviously enjoyed exercising his pen in these attacks, for he gleefully welcomes an occasion for a poem on Rivington: once it is the faultiness of the type in Rivington's paper, once it is the use of new types, and once the use of a new engraving of the king's arms on the masthead (for which, Freneau avers, Satan anointed Rivington " 'The Inventor as well as the Printer of lies' "). But Freneau really did not need faults in the format of Rivington's paper to inspire him; lacking an occasion, he could create one, as in "Rivington's Last Will and Testament," "Rivington's Reflections," and "Rivington's Confessions"—all of which emphasize the printer's capacity for lies. Each pretends to be autobiographical: through the series Freneau shows Rivington deciding to go over to the rebels, confident of their mercy; for, "if they spare us for Murder they'll spare us for Lying."

A better poem using a similar device is "Political Biography: Hugh Gaine's Life." Through Gaine, a New York Tory printer, Freneau satirizes himself and other New Yorkers; but he also presents his fears for the future. Like the later Rivington poems, Freneau has Gaine, in asking for tolerance from the Whigs, summarize the history of the struggle as he knows it, or as he would now like it known. Gaine describes his actions before the war broke out: "Yes, I was a whig, and a whig from my heart,/ But still was unwilling with Britain to part." He is not quite clear about which of his deeds he should be excusing to the Tories and which to the rebels, for he apologizes for printing Whig poetry: "to gain a mere trifle, a shilling or so,/ I printed some treason for Philip Freneau." (This verse Gaine describes as "so full of invective, and loaded with spleen,/ So sneeringly smart, and so hellishly keen.") Gaine describes his flight at first from the British to the Jerseys and then the reason for his return to the British: "meeting misfortunes and endless disasters,/ And forced to submit to a hundred new masters,/ I thought it more prudent to hold to the one."

Freneau's opinion of the efficiency of the committees and congresses is evidently not high—nor are his expectations for the postwar period high, as Gaine describes the future:

> Who knows but, in time, I may rise to be great,
> And have the good fortune to manage a State?
> Great noise among people great changes denotes,
> And I shall have money to purchase their votes—
> The time is approaching, I venture to say,
> When folks worse than me will come into play
> The false-hearted Tory will give themselves airs,
> And aim to take hold of the helm of affairs,
> While the honest bold soldier, who sought your renown,
> Like a dog in the dirt, shall be crushed and held down.
> Of honours and profits allow me a share!

Gaine, as pictured by Freneau, is not a sly or politic man; despite his political sins, he remains an engaging poetic character.

In great contrast to Freneau's description of Gaine as a bumbling, naive man is his characterization, late in the war, of Lord Cornwallis. Of the British commanders in America, Freneau's strongest verse is reserved for him. "To Lord Cornwallis" begins "Hail, great destroyer (equalled yet by none)/ Of countries not your master's, nor your own." Freneau describes him as the son of a devil and then labels him "the plundering servant of a bankrupt king." The more grisly "On the Fall of General Earl Cornwallis" was written after the surrender; and this poem does not celebrate the American triumph but rejoices in Cornwallis' fall. "Monster" is one of the milder terms Freneau uses to describe Cornwallis: he is a "man of hell," who should, like Cain, be branded: "he with a brother's blood his hands did stain,/ One brother he, you have a thousand slain." Freneau cannot describe Cornwallis' misdeeds strongly enough: "Alone he stood, arch-butcher of the times,/ Rov'd uncontroul'd this wasted country o'er,/ Strew'd plains with dead, and bathed his jaws with gore." Freneau reaches his climax of anger when he advises Cornwallis to end his destructive life, and he also wishes a miserable end for the king: "So may destruction rush with speedy wing,/ Low as yourself, to drag your cruel king;/ His head torn off, his hands, his feet, and all,/ Deep in the dust may Dagon's image fall." This poem is, however, an exception to Freneau's war poems; usually, the British are pictured, like Gaine, as weak and vacillating: credulous, incompetent, they have misplaced values.

Freneau had little occasion to celebrate American feats of arms, either on sea or land; but he did recall to his public the victory of John Paul Jones with two poems, "Captain Jones' Invitation" (1786) and "On the Memorable Victory" (1781). The latter, although it chronicles the events of the battle, lacks the realism of the battle between the *Aurora* and *Iris* in "The British Prison Ship." In "On the Memorable Victory," the lines "Down, prostrate down, the Britons fall,/ The decks were strew'd with slain" do not carry the urgency of the battle, nor do such reflections as "Alas! that e'er the god decreed/ That brother should by brother bleed" speed the chronicle. "Captain Jones's Invitation" is, however, a success. It is a sea song with heavy rhythm and a strong, one-line refrain. In it, Jones is calling for men to join him in his cruise:

> If thou has courage to despise
> The various changes of the skies,
> To disregard the ocean's rage,
> Unmov'd when hostile ships engage,
> Come from thy forest, and with me
> Learn what it is to go to sea.

Freneau had another opportunity to celebrate sea exploits when the Philadelphia merchants banded together to outfit a ship to discourage British and Tory privateers from preying on their shipping. The ship, the *Hyder Ally*, was given to the command of Captain Barney; and, on April 9, 1782, he triumphed over the British *General Monk*. Freneau reported poetically on these events in "On the Late Royal Sloop of War General Monk," in "Barney's Invitation" ("Attend, my lads, to honour's call,/ Embark in our

Hyder Ali "), and in "Song: On Captain Barney's Victory over the Ship General Monk"—all written in 1782. In the third poem, Freneau, working with a shorter line than usual, created a rollicking history of the event; speeches are given to both captains, and each is determined to worst the other. Barney, of course, succeeds; and Freneau concludes: "Thus be Britain's woes completed,/ Thus abriged her cruel reign,/ 'Till she ever, thus defeated,/ Yields the sceptre of the main."

One of Freneau's rare poems dealing with American land engagements is also his most famous: "To the Memory of the Brave Americans " (1781) celebrates Greene's battle at Eutaw Springs. Eutaw Springs, although not a victory, gave the Americans a sense of pride because the rebel lines not only held for a while in the face of seasoned British troops but also inflicted heavy damages on them. Freneau's poem, while mourning those who died, exults in the rebels' bravery and courage. Because of this pride, the poem is saved from being just another melancholy elegy, a class in which the following lines might place it:

> Weep on, ye springs, your tearful tide;
> How many heroes are no more!
>
> O smite your gentle breast, and say
> The friends of freedom slumber here!
>
> Sigh for the wasted rural reign;
> Sigh for the shepherds, sunk to rest!

There are, however, other more inspiring lines. Greene's troops "saw their injured country's woe;/ The flaming town, the wasted field;/ Then rushed to meet the insulting foe." But the Britons, "full as bold,/ Retreated, and retreating slew." The final stanza asks that "our patriot band" rest in peace after their labors: "We trust they find a happier land,/ A brighter sunshine of their own." The poem is frankly sentimental — and frankly patriotic in its celebration of the heroes.

Of all the American heroes, the one to receive the most praise from Freneau was Washington. "To his Excellency General Washington," printed in September, 1781, extolls Washington's steadfastness in the face of defeat and his achievements at Boston and New Jersey. Freneau tells Washington of the worldwide fame he has, and he wishes continued conquests for his future and a peaceful death late in life. Two years later, on December 10, 1783, Freneau published "Verses Occasioned by General Washington's arrival in Philadelphia, on his way to his seat in Virginia." Although Freneau again repeats the theme of Washington's fame, the poem centers on praise of Washington's decision to retire and on a description of his ideal future:

> Freedom shall still employ your mind,
> Slavery shall vanish, wide and far,
> 'Till not a trace is left behind;
> Your counsels not bestow'd in vain
> Shall still protect this infant reign.

The war over, Freneau looked ahead to postwar achievements.

V   *Poems on the War of 1812*

By the War of 1812, Freneau had himself retired; now a gentleman farmer, he lived quietly in New Jersey with an occasional visit to New York. Perhaps as a result, his occasional verse about the War of 1812 does not carry the excitement of that written about the Revolutionary War. The 1812 verse is almost sedate; it is more carefully composed, more carefully thought out. The impression given by most of these poems is that Freneau wrote them almost out of obligation because the events of the war were the news of the day. This war, having come, had to be fought; the troops, to be cheered; the heroes, to be praised. But the almost rabid propaganda of the earlier poems does not appear—only a few of the poems come close to having the fire of the earlier ones. Although these later poems are technically better, they lack the power of immediacy of the first war poems.

A good example of Freneau's comparatively sedate approach to the War of 1812 is "On the Symptoms of Hostilities," which begins "but will they once more be engaged in a war,/ Be fated to discord again?" Then the poet asks, "and who is to blame? . . ./ Did nature predestine this curse to mankind;/ Or is it the cruel destestable task/ That tyrants impose, with their minions combined?" Freneau, of course, concludes that the tyrants are indeed to blame; but, instead of attacking a specific king, Freneau adopts his later and more general position that all nondemocratic governments lead their people continually to war. Freneau is but repeating a long-held belief when he states that "to reason with tyrants is surely absurd;/ To argue with them is to preach to the deaf:/ They argue alone by the length of the sword;/ Their honor the same as the word of a thief." How mildly Freneau presents this *ad hominem* argument in contrast with his earlier poems!

Perhaps the nature of Freneau's 1812 verse is different because of the nature of the war. Few thought that Britain was intending to conquer the United States; few thought that it could be conquered. The issue during the Revolutionary War was a grave one, and the outcome was doubtful; but in the War of 1812 the existence of the new nation was not at stake. Although in "To America" Freneau wishes for the day when Britain will "to her hell return," the satanic imagery which he used to describe the British in his Revolutionary War verse is only rarely present. Freneau no longer saw wars as black-white battles.

It would be going too far to say that Freneau viewed the war objectively—occasionally, his spleen is vented in verse, but rarely so. In his best war poems, Freneau takes an amused, detached view of the common soldier; he shows him to be neither a hero nor a villain; he is, like any man, as liable to fault in wartime as in peacetime. "Military Recruiting" is somewhat inappropriately named, for the bulk of the poem celebrates cigar smoking: "old care I dismiss'd/ While I held in my fist/ The pitcher, and smoked the segar." Only the last three stanzas connect it to the war: the sailor needs the cigar to make his duties bearable; and the untried soldier "would stand to his cannon, firm as a rock/ Would they let him but smoke his segar." In Freneau's Revolutionary War poems, there were no untested soldiers; such lures as drink and cigars were unnecessary then. Another picture of the common soldier is "The Suttler and the Soldier," the bulk of which is a monologue by the sutler, acting as bartender, who is selling brandy to a young soldier. The sutler, a veteran, presents a soldier's life in detail:

> "To live, for months on scanty fare,
> To sleep, by night in open air,
> To fight, and every danger share;
> All these await.

> "But bear them all!—wherever led,
> And live contented, though half fed:—
> A couch of straw, and canvas shed
> Shall be your fate!"

The sergeant finally intervenes; his man has grown tipsy—but the sutler has achieved his purpose—he has sold his product. "The Suttler and the Soldier" is not a call to arms, not a record of a battle won or lost, but a picture of a garrulous bartender, in wartime, who gives a realistic picture of war.

A more humorous poem showing the everyday in time of war is "The Parade and Sham-Fight" in which Freneau describes the local militia going through its exercises while being directed by a commander with dreams of glory but little experience. Caped with a blanket, armed with a sword and two pistols, the commander gives his orders:

> Accoutered thus, with martial air,
> He gave the warning word, "Take care!"
> And, in a moment, all was war,
> Sublime and grand.
>
> They march'd, and march'd, as thick as bees,
> Then march'd towards a clump of trees;
> And "blaze away!" the leader says—
> "Each take his aim!
>
> "Who wounds a tree can kill a man—
> If you but practice on that plan,
> The britons shall go home again
> With grief and shame!"

Freneau continues to describe the day's activities in mock-heroic style, and the tragedy of the day occurs when one of the men steals the keg of brandy intended for all. This type of verse is what we may expect from Freneau in his later years; for, no longer a participant or an enthusiast, he can be detached. Moreover, the fate of his country did not hang in the balance.

Freneau's treatment of the British in his poetry of the War of 1812 is less radical than that of the revolutionary war. His language is more temperate; his insults are fairer. In essence, he is no longer purely the propagandist whose intent is to picture the enemy as everything mean and vile. In the poem "The Battle of Lake Erie," the British commander, Barclay, is motivated, according to Freneau, by ambition and "royal smiles" but not by Satan. The British sailors are shown as worthy opponents: "For never yet braver band/ To fight a ship, forsook the land,/ Than Barclay had on board that day." The very mildness of the concluding stanza is interesting:

> Thus, for dominion of the lake
> These captains did each other rake,
> And many a widow did they make;—
> Whose is the fault, or who to blame?—
> The briton challenged with his sword,
> The yankee took him at his word,
> With spirit laid him close on board—
> They're ours—he said—and closed the game.

The Freneau of the Revolution would never have thought to question who was to blame, even rhetorically. To the earlier Freneau, the blame was too clearly that of the British to need questioning.

Despite Freneau's muted verse about this war, he again attacked British royalty. In both "On the British Invasion" and in the following from "Royal Consultations," the royal family is pictured as debating what to do with "Wellington's ten thousand slaves":

> Said the goth to the vandal, the prince to the king,
> Let us do a mad action, to make the world ring:
> With Wellington's army we now have the means
> To make a bold stroke and exhibit new scenes.
>
> A stroke at the states is my ardent desire,
> To waste, and harass them with famine and fire;
> My vengeance to carry through village and town,
> And even to batter their capitol down.

Freneau's heavy rhythm enhances the poem by giving, somehow, the whole discussion an air of frivolity. Despite the name-calling and the harsh words, it is almost a good-humored poem. Freneau is laughing at the enemy.

Freneau often belittled the British by using humor or by making them appear ridiculous. In "Sir Peter Petrified," he chronicles a serious battle by describing it as an attempt by the British to steal geese from a Maryland farmer who was able to repulse the troops and kill the commander. In "On the Conflagrations at Washington," he is at great pains to show the silliness of British logic. The action itself is described in serious terms: "Six thousand heroes disembark—/ Each left at night his floating ark/ And Washington was made their mark." But, after recording the success of these grand preparations, Freneau mocks the achievement:

> To conquer armies in the field
> Was, once, the surest method held
> To make a hostile country yield.
> The mode is this, now acted on;
> In conflagrating Washington,
> They held our independence gone!

Freneau's "distance" from this war is revealed by his very lightness, now shown especially in the way he phrases his farewell to the Washington buildings:

> They left our congress naked walls—
> Farewell to towers and capitols!
> To lofty roofs and splendid halls!
>
> To courtly domes and glittering things,
> To folly, that too near us clings,
> To courtiers who—'tis well—had wings.

This verse is not that of a nationalist who is outraged by the desecration of his country's capital. Freneau had indeed mellowed.

Perhaps the best of Freneau's poems written about the War of 1812 is "The Terrific Torpedoes." It illustrates Freneau's sense of humor which leavens—indeed, almost gets the better of—his patriotic purpose. The poem's ostensible goal is to depict the cowardice of the British (typified by one Sir Thomas Hardy) when faced by Robert Fulton's invention, the torpedo. Fortunately, Hardy escapes the author's patriotic purpose; and the poem becomes a humorous portrayal of the commander's facing battle. In enjoying the picture of Sir Thomas, we forget that he is The Enemy. Sir Thomas' monologue begins with an almost Shakespearean diatribe against Fulton which questions his humanity:

> Was you, an infant, to a mother press'd
> Or did ferocious tigers give the breast—
> Did nature in some angry moment plan
> Some fierce hyena to degrade the man?
> Resolve me quick, for doubtful while I stay
> These dark torpedoes may be on their way.

After this bombastic beginning, Sir Thomas more quietly, almost muttering to himself, complains of being unable to sleep because of

his fear of the unseen torpedo. He denies vigorously the reports that
he has slept: "The chaplain said he heard me snore,/ But many a fib
he told before;/ And if I snored, I'm satisfied/ 'Twas when my eyes
were open wide." After this digression, Hardy returns to the
thought of the torpedo, the infernal machine, and of how nervous it
has made him. Of course, he pictures the effect of the torpedo's
success: "In scatter'd fragments to the sky/ This ship of ships will
clattering fly." What then will happen to him, to his men, to "the
pretty maid/ That sweeps my floor and makes my bed?" Perhaps,
thinks Sir Thomas, the pretty maid can provide consolation:

> Do, Fanny, go and boil some tea:
> Come hither, love, and comfort me:
> A glass of wine! my spirits sink!
> The last perhaps that I shall drink!—
> Or go—unlock the brandy case
> And let us have a dram a piece;—
> No matter if your nose is red,
> We shall be sober when we're dead.

The progression in these few lines from tea to wine to brandy is an
admirable device to represent the growing terror of the man. After
this point, Hardy accepts his impending doom, complaining only
that he has in all other battles stood fast; Fulton's art alone has made
him a coward. Englishmen, he implies, would not use such inhu-
man devices. Finally, in facing his fate, he describes to Fanny the
future state:

> Where all is love, and no one hates;
> No falling kings or rising states;
> No colors that we must defend,
> If sick, or dead, or near our end;
> Where yankees are admitted not
> To hatch their damn'd torpedo plot:
> Where you will have no beds to make,
> Nor I be doom'd to lie awake.

By the conclusion of the poem, we feel a certain sympathy for poor
Sir Thomas.

Freneau's light tone, indicating his refusal to take the war seriously, persists in his recording of events both early and late in the
war. In "The Battle of Stonington," he says the British objective was

to steal some sheep; but he depicts the natives of the threatened
town hardly more heroically:

> A deacon, then popp'd up his head
> And parson Jones's sermon read,
> In which the reverend doctor said
> That they must fight for Stonington.
>
> A townsman bade them, next, attend
> To sundry resolutions penn'd,
> By which they promised to defend
> With sword and gun, old Stonington.

Few wits in the Middle States ever let an opportunity escape them
to satirize the customs of New England, and Freneau is no exception. But the Yankees defended their fort, and the British began
their attack: "They kill'd a goose, they kill'd a hen,/ Three hogs they
wounded in a pen—/ They dash'd away, and pray what then?/ This
was not taking Stonington." We cannot help feeling that Freneau
enjoyed this war. His remoteness from it is indicated in almost
every poem he wrote about it.

Only when he wrote of the occasions of naval battles does his
verse seem reminiscent of that of the Revolutionary War. In "The
Battle of Lake Champlain," which records Thomas Macdonough's
victory, Macdonough is described as a hero all could admire:

> He stood amidst Columbia's sons,
> He stood amidst dismounted guns,
> He fought amidst heart-rendering groans,
> The tatter'd sail, the tottering mast.

It is not often that Freneau celebrated an action so enthusiastically;
conversely, rarely does he chastise the British vigorously. When he
does, it is likely to be when describing a naval action. "On the Loss
of the Privateer Brigantine" records Freneau's indignation about the
loss which occurred when the British invaded a neutral port to take
the *General Armstrong*. This deed brought Freneau to express at
last his ire:

> Of neutrals what nonsense some tell us each day!
> Exists there a neutral where Britain has sway?
> The rights of a neutral!—away with such stuff—

> What neutral remains that can England rebuff?—
> To be safe from disgrace
> The deep seas are our place:
> The flag of no neutral our flag can defend,
> By ourselves we must fight, on ourselves must depend.

This verse—direct, idiomatic—shows that Freneau still retained his stylistic vigor and that some events could prod him from his pose of quiet amusement about the events of this war.

VI   *Poems of Controversy*

Since Freneau seems to have always had a clear conception of the ideal way men and governments should act, and, since the reality rarely met the ideal, many of his poems comment about this discrepancy. After the Revolutionary War's successful conclusion, Freneau was quick to point out the faults of the postwar leaders and their policies. The new leaders were no longer heroes, revolutionary triumph led to party squabbling, and the democratic French republic degenerated into Napoleon's Empire. Although some of Freneau's poems reflect his bitterness at what he thought were reverses of progress, the poems were not written to express bitterness *per se* but to educate, to reiterate the ideal, to warn. Thus, while recording wrongs, Freneau always indicates the possibility of right.

Although Freneau avoids criticism in his war verse of rebel bureaucracy and bungling, he did become a partisan in a Pennsylvania political battle waged in 1782. The *Freeman's Journal* and Freneau favored the Constitutionalists and General Joseph Reed, whereas the *Independent Gazetter* favored the conservative John Dickinson. A writer for the *Independent Gazetter*, signing himself "A Foe to Tyrants," attacked Freneau, accusing him of slander. In his own verse, Freneau did not defend the party or the issues but attacked his opponent's verse, as in "To The Concealed Royalist. On His Farewell": "In his own lines he tolled his funeral bell,/ And when he could not sing—he stunk—farewell!" In Freneau's "New Year's Verses" for 1783, he refers to the quarrel; and he piously hopes that such bickering will "disgrace our rising State no more." "On the Death of the Republican Patriot and Statesman, General Joseph Reed," printed in the *Freeman's Journal* of March 9, 1785, mourns the death not only of Reed but of the many patriotic and virtuous leaders of the Revolution. The poem concludes: "REED, rest in peace: for time's impartial page/ Shall blast the wrongs of this ungrateful age." I doubt that this particular party battle either embittered Freneau markedly or made him a cynic. It probably did, however, emphasize the fact that, although the revolution was achieved, the nature of man would not change, nor would the new political process always produce satisfaction.

Two poems, written at the close of the war, indicate that ambition is the ruling motive of man; consequently, the poems are quite pessimistic. One, "The Projectors," deals with the speculation in western lands. In it, Freneau recalls early times, when each man was content to till his own soil. Now, "it is a truth well understood,/ 'All would be tyrants if they could.' " And Freneau, as his solution, advocates a return to the early Roman virtue of moderation. Later, he printed "The Prophecy of King Tammany," a curious blend of portrayal of the "noble savage" and of complaint about the evil of modern times. Tammany, complaining of the Europeans' incursion into his land, sees his revenge in the future after the British are defeated:

> "A sordid race will then succeed,
> To slight the virtues of the firmer race,
> That brought your tyrant to disgrace,
> Shall give your honours to an odious train,
> Who shunned all conflicts on the main
> And dared no battles on the bloody plain,
> Whose little souls sunk in the gloomy day
> When virtue only could support the fray
> And sunshine friends kept off—or ran away."

For purposes of his criticism, Freneau used the past—recent revolutionary or ancient Roman—as the ideal. Still, his faith that the future would bring a better man remained constant.

Freneau celebrated every step taken in the United States or in Europe away from monarchy, and he deplored every new monarchical tendency. Thus, his poem "On the Proposed System of State Consolidation" is filled with dire forebodings: the plan (to unite the states under one government) was conceived by "misguided men," who "held a prostituted pen," who "from monstrous creeds a monstrous system drew." The plan, while in itself mild, indicates a deeper sickness in the nation: "In ten short years, of freedom weary grown,/ The state, republic, sickens for a throne;/

Senates and sycophants a pattern bring/ A mere disguise for parliament and king." Freneau warns the honest common people that,
"when thirteen states are moulded into one,/ Your rights are vanish'd and your glory gone." This style is, of course, typical of
Freneau's propagandistic one; for he exaggerates and magnifies the
perceived wrong. He also uses ridicule, as in his answer to the
charge by the Federalists that the Democratic editors were paid by
France to defend France and to promote the ideals of the French
Revolution. "To the Democratic Country Editors" begins by seeming to accept the charges: "You, Journalists, are bribed—that's
clear,/ And paid French millions by the year;/ We see it in the coats
you wear." But then, after pointing out the obvious poverty of the
Democratic editors, Freneau reminds them, "why did you not with
Tories join/ To hold the British king divine—/ . . . / Then had your
faces shined with fat—/ Then had you worn the gold-laced hat." As it
is, the poor editors cannot collect from their patrons; and, in addition, they face fines and jail under the Alien and Sedition laws. By
ridiculing and exaggerating the Federalists' charge, Freneau ef-
fectively defends the editors.

The best known of Freneau's poems written on the events of John
Adams' administration is probably "Stanzas to An Alien," which is
addressed to John Burk, the Democratic editor who was fined and
jailed and who fled New York to avoid additional imprisonment. In
this poem, Freneau adopts the weary tone appropriate for mourning
the passage of republican virtue:

> Remote, beneath a sultry star,
> Where Mississippi flows afar,
> I see you rambling, God knows where.
>
> Sometimes, beneath a cypress bough,
> When met in dreams, with spirits low,
> I long to tell you what I know.
>
> How matters go, in this our day,
> When monarchy renews her sway,
> And royalty begins her play.

The mourning tone continues as Freneau contrasts Burk's present
freedom with his own situation: "Where I must stay, no joys are
found;/ Excisemen haunt the hateful ground." Finally, the tone

shifts slightly in "perdition seize that odious race," but the poem has
no hope that the monarchical tendency will be cured. "Stanzas to An
Alien" is perhaps the most mournful occasional poem written by
Freneau. More restrained in expressing his disappointment with
the *status quo*, it is also more effective.

But, even while events at home caused Freneau distress, he was
able to record with a more cheerful tone some events in Europe
which seemed to indicate that republican virtues would soon win
ascendancy there. "On the Invasion of Rome" (1797) and "On the
Death of Catharine II" (1815) represent the positive and negative
aspects of the same feeling. The first poem celebrates the legions of
the French Republic for "liberating" Italy: "May each new conquest
all the past transcend,/ Still may those hosts their first great plan
pursue,/ And honor, freedom, virtue keep in view." Catharine, for
Freneau, represented the past, "that iron sway/ Which bids the
brute, not man, obey." She is described as a "female wolf, whom
wolves did nurse," who "fear'd the savage from the den/ Would see
and learn the rights of men." The poem, in essence, celebrates
Catharine's death and predicts that, if her successor sends armies
against France, they will fail.

For Freneau, the French Republic did not remain virtuous for
long and in one of his last poems, one simply titled "Bonaparte," he
predicts Napoleon's downfall for having subverted the ideals of the
Republic. Napoleon, Freneau says, is now on high, but fortune will
soon change:

> For round him *dogs* unnumbered growl,
> And distant *wolves*, still louder, howl,
> And *vultures* scream, and *tigers* roar;
> And nations are disgusted more
> With *regal rank* that he assumes;
> More rancour boils within the breast,
> And more this sudden change detest
> Than human wisdom overcomes!

He will deserve his disaster, for "he swore to keep a nation free/
That had relapsed to anarchy,/ He swore to guard democracy,/ Not
hurl it down, not hurl it down!" As in this poem, Freneau rarely
recorded simply an event; he connected it with his own hopes and
aspirations. The poem fully reveals his disappointment.

If Freneau were disappointed with the reality of current events, he was also disappointed with the cultural atmosphere of America. In "Epistle to Sylvius: On the Folly of Writing Poetry" (1786), he complains: "Low in the dust is genius laid,/ The muses with the man in trade." He is driven to condemn poets for expecting too much of mankind: "To mend the world, is still their aim:/ The world, alas! remains the same,/ And so must stand to every age,/ Proof to the morals of the page!" The poet is a fool to try to improve mankind, especially through poetry published in a land that has no appreciation for it. Although Freneau generally praises Reason, he finds its dominance in the new republic discouraging to poetic fancy. In "To An Author," he proves that

> On these bleak climes by Fortune thrown,
> Where rigid Reason reigns alone,
> Where lovely Fancy has no sway,
> Nor magic forms around her play—
> Nor nature takes her summer hue
> Tell me, what has the muse to do?—
>
> An age employed in edging steel
> Can no poetic raptures feel.

Nathaniel Hawthorne and the Romantics were not the first to complain about the unreceptive American atmosphere:

One could do little about the temper of the times, but Freneau did feel that patriotism should extend to American literary products. As "Robert Slender," essayist, Freneau commented somewhat wryly about the dominance of British authors: "They are, however, excuseable in treating the American authors as inferiors; a political and literary independence of their nation being two very different things—the first was accomplished in about seven years, the latter will not be completely effected, perhaps, in as many centuries."[10] But, as a poet aroused by a current event, Freneau was capable of stronger, less philosophical attitudes. In "Literary Importation," the immediate event was the appointment of an American Episcopal Bishop; before the war, the appointment had been potent propaganda for independence. Now, independence won, most took the appointment in stride. But Freneau regarded it as only another instance of a dire trend:

> It seems we had spirit to humble a throne,
> Have genius for science inferior to none,

> But hardly encourage a plant of our own:
> > If a college be planned,
> > 'Tis all at a stand
> 'Till to Europe we send at a shameful expanse,
> To send us a book-worm to teach us some sense.

So Freneau turns his back on European culture: there are also implications in the poem of the value of "common sense" over "book-learning"—an unusual position for Freneau, the poet and the scholar.

But the arts were not alone in their suffering. Freneau supported John Churchman's application to Congress for funds to study magnetic fields, a study which would greatly aid seafaring. In "To Mr. Churchman" (1791), Freneau adopts a mocking persona who tells Churchman, " 'tis your own fault if you repine!/ You should have mention'd some rich golden mine." Avarice rules over the arts and sciences in the councils, for their members, "tho' willing to be thought prodigious scholars," care little for such projects. In "To Memmius" (1791), Freneau returns to the same theme. Churchman's project was just practical enough to succeed, but the favorites of the councils are the bridge builders and steamship inventors. Poets and litterateurs must inevitably lose the patronage battle: " 'Nothing but useful projects we require,'/ (Cries a new-fangled, self-important 'squire)."

But, though Freneau complained poetically about the neglect of the arts and sciences, he was as pleased as the rest of his countrymen with their achievements in "useful projects." One of his more notable later occasional poems, "The Great Western Canal" (1821), celebrates the Erie Canal and its promoters: "Ye Prompters of a work so vast/ That may for years, for centuries last;/ Where Nature tried to bar the way/ You mark'd her steps, but changed her sway." And the practical inventor is singled out for praise in a late elegy, "On the Death of Robert Fulton" (1823). Fulton is praised for giving to mankind "at once the USEFUL, GREAT, and NEW." Freneau is enough of an American to praise utility; he is enough of a poet to protest the emphasis on it.

Although Freneau was intrigued with balloons, it was on the question of their utility that he mocked them. Part of him would have totally approved that section of Jonathan Swift's *Gulliver's Travels* which satirizes the Royal Academy and its theoretical scientific pursuits. On the occasion of a balloon demonstration, Freneau wrote "The Progress of Balloons" (1784). In this poem, he allowed his fancy to go wild as he cataloged possible practical applications of balloons, which to him were apparently quite ridiculous. He hypothesizes their use as a means of transportation, of delivering the mail, of exploring the planets ("In Saturn, advise us if snow ever melts,/ And what are the uses of Jupiter's belts"), of carrying cargoes of farm products, of carrying on warfare:

> If Britain should ever disturb us again,
> (As they threaten to do in the next George's reign)
> No doubt they will play us a set of new tunes,
> And pepper us well from their fighting balloons.

However, Freneau also admired the science of balloons; he wrote several poems praising one experimenter, Mr. Blanchard. Freneau's fancy and curiosity often led him to take contradictory positions about minor subjects.

VII *Poems of Everyday Occasions*

One of Freneau's longest—and most popular—poems celebrates the common man who is experiencing what was for many an everyday event, but which is to the characters in the poem an extraordinary one. "A Journey from Philadelphia to New York" (1787) is ostensibly written by one Robert Slender, a weaver of Philadelphia. The poem consists of initial depiction of the travelers, their argument about which is the best way to go, the mishaps they encounter along the way, and finally their arrival at New York. The journey has long been a literary device used to explore character; but, unlike other picaresque pieces, Freneau does not continually introduce new characters; his attention stays with the original cast. The poem maintains constant good humor—the follies of the travelers are shown sympathetically and as being those common to every man.

Robert Slender claims the journey began with his desire for fresh air and for escape from his loom. In developing Slender's need for fresh air, Freneau gives what may be one of the first commentaries about American suburbs:

> Our citizens think, when they sit themselves down
> In the gardens that grow in the skirts of the town,
> They think they have got in some rural retreat,

> Where the nymphs of the groves, and the singing birds meet
> When only a fence shuts them out from the street;
> With the smoke of the city be-clouding their eyes
> They sit in their boxes, and look very wise,
> Take a sip of bad punch, or a glass of sour wine;
> Conceiting their pleasures are equal to mine,
> Who rove where I will, and wherever I roam,
> In spite of new faces, am always at home.

The last two lines of the quotation express the ideal of the Enlightened universal man who is at home everywhere because man everywhere is similar. But the group Slender gathers is a varied one, even though its members are common types. There are William Snip, tailor; his wife, a shrew; and their silly apprentice. There are also Captain O'Keef, a blustery soldier; his companion of the moment, Cynthia, a milliner's girl; Toupee, a French hairdresser, whose only thought is to turn the journey into profit for himself; and Bob, a ballad singer, who "had sung for the great and had rhym'd for the small,/ But scarcely a shilling had got by them all." The last two travelers are Ezekiel, a Rhode Island lawyer, and Brian O'Bluster, a seaman, much given to girls and grog.

Throughout the journey, these characters react as types; there are no surprising character revelations. The greatest excitement comes after the group transfers to a carriage, which promptly overturns, leaving everyone bruised—Will Snip certain that he is dying. But Snip survives, and the travelers finish their journey on a boat on which everyone, including the soldier, becomes sick: "And you, Robert Slender, were not at your ease;/ Yet couldn't help laughing at captain O'Keef,/ Who shunn'd little Cynthia, and cast up his beef." The poem is not a delicate one. Although Freneau omitted this dialogue in his 1809 revision, a salty exchange occurs between the packet captain and the seaman in the 1787 version. The captain ridicules the seaman with a long catalog of nautical terms (all in perfect couplets), and then O'Bluster has his turn:

> "You ague-cheek'd, cream-coulour'd son of a bitch,
> Who have sail'd all your life on a fresh-water ditch,
> Whose mate (answer'd Billy) might be an old wife,
> Who never have rattled a shroud in your life,
> Whose guts would come up if the ship were in motion,
> Whose barque never look'd at the foam of the ocean."

To quiet this outburst, the fresh-water skipper gives O'Bluster grog.
The poem celebrates the harmless but humorous failings of the
common man—Slender does not look down upon or sneer at any
one of them. As we might expect, the poem was popular with
Freneau's contemporaries. A poem of fancy, "A Journey from
Philadelphia to New York" catches real character traits; and the
incidents, while humorous, are believable.

Freneau could apply his poetic fancy to the most trivial occasions
and make them entertaining. A few of the better poems of this type
are "Address to a Learned Pig" (1797), "Elegiac Verses on the Death
of a Favourite Dog" (1785), "On Finding a Terrapin in the Woods,
Which Had A.D. 1756 Marked on the Back of his Shell" (1815), and
"Stanzas Occasioned by a Melancholy Survey of an Old English
Tobacco Box Inscribed 1708" (1809). In "The Literary Plunder-
ers" (1785), Freneau expresses his consternation at finding his favorite volumes nibbled by mice, and he sounds the theme of encour-
agement of the arts and sciences in a humorous way:

> To arms, to arms! Ye chosen few
> Who science love, and arts pursue;
> Or, if your arms should nought avail,
> (Since mice may over men prevail)
> Put on some wise, inventive cap,
> AND FIND US A COMPLETER TRAP.

One of the more enjoyable of these lighter occasional poems is "To
the Dog Sancho, on His being Wounded in the Head with a Sabre,
in a Midnight Assault and Robbery, near the Neversink Hills,
1778." The poem begins with the poet's generalizing about the
incident: "The world, my dear Sancho, is full of distress,/ And you
have your share, I allow and confess." Then the poet retells the
incident—the dog is barking, the robbery. Finally, the poet promises the dog his rewards:

> I'll give him a verse with the GREAT of the age,
> And if he quite dies, he must die in my page;
> And long may he live in despite of the mob,
> And the *fools*, who his master, a poet, would rob.
>
> Wherever I take up my evening retreat,
> Dear Sancho, I'll have you to lie at my feet;

> And whether at home, or in regions remote
> For a bed, I'll allot you the skirts of a coat.

The incident is minor, but the treatment is imaginative. Although these light poems are neither significant nor weighty, nor important in the history of verse or nation, they do, I think, reflect the man who can turn his fancy to any subject, no matter how small, and who feels at ease doing so. In Freneau's world, all subjects are worthy ones.

For many of his responses to minor current events, however, fancy is secondary to protest. For example, Freneau did not find frontier life ideal; the customs and living conditions of the frontier, he complained, were uncouth and boorish. When South Carolina decided to move the capital from Charleston to Columbia, in the interior, Freneau enjoyed himself in a series of poems written in 1789 by predicting the fright the bears and wolves roaming the backwoods streets would cause, and how the elegant legislators would turn into rustics:

> Dull, melancholy streams,
> Dutch politics and schemes,
> Owls screeching in the empty street—
> Wolves howling at the doors—
> Bears breaking into stores;
> These make the picture of the town—complete.

Another visit to the backwoods led Freneau to record the event of a gouging. "The Gougers" (1809) illustrates Freneau's habit of protesting in verse any action that shocked him, no matter how unpoetic the subject might be thought. The poem, "On Seeing a Traveller Gouged, and Otherwise Ill Treated by Some Citizens of Log Town, Near a Pine Barren," shows Freneau's spleen overcoming his detachment:

> Was it the part of honest men
> Who bear the name of citizen,
> On a poor stranger thus to fall,
> And sightless make his visual ball?—
> Who first such savage warfare taught,
> His heart was out of marble wrought.

When witnessing events like these, Freneau continues, he regrets his function as a poet: "Why do I hold so dull a pen/ To satirize ferocious men;—/ Why is it not impelled, in force/ To give such bosoms their remorse." Fated, however, to wield his pen as a writing instrument, instead of as a battle weapon, Freneau uses it to compose a curse on the town and townsmen. For Freneau, the frontier was not romantic.

Despite the realism of his minor occasional poems, with their graphic and sometimes grotesque details, Freneau clung to his vision of the general progress of men. In "On the Prospect of a Revolution in France" (1790), Freneau reaffirms his ideal:

> Flushed with new life, and brightening at the view,
> Genius, triumphant, moulds the world anew;
> To these far climes in swift succession moves
> Each art that Reason owns and sense approves.

It is this ideal that explains most of Freneau's poetic reactions to events. The ideal of the progress of Reason persists; and, when events do not conform to it or promote it, Freneau strikes out, shows men where they are in error, protests in any way he feels will be effective—sarcastically, humorously, indignantly or fancifully. Of all his occasional verse, most are, in some way, "protest" poems. Among the exceptions are his sea poems, although even in them he has something to say about the nature of man and about how he should cope philosophically with his environment. The ideal he held to was common among the thinkers of the Enlightenment; his study of man was to be for the benefit of man. Although he occasionally expresses himself as longing for quiet retreats away from man, or for conditions where the arts would dwell supreme, he was essentially a cosmopolitan who liked the turmoils created by man and the opportunity they offered for a study of man's nature.

CHAPTER 3

Prose: Newspapers and Essays

THE ten years from 1790 to 1800 were the most active and public ones of Freneau's life. Although he showed during these years a marked desire to settle down in New Jersey, national events called him forth to employ his talents, ones shown earlier with the *Freeman's Journal*, as a newspaper editor and political essayist. Although he published one book of verse, printing himself the 1795 *Poems, Written between the years 1768 and 1794*, his poetry was generally written and published only to emphasize his editorial stands. In these years he married, reared a family, moved from New York to Philadelphia to New Jersey and back to New York. He retained his former intellectual interests and causes: he continued to champion debtors, to abhor slavery, to speculate about just treatment of the Indians, to admire the French, and to question established religion.

His political friendship belonged nationally to the Jeffersonian Republicans and locally to the New York Clintonians and Pennsylvania radicals. His talents were sought by three future presidents, James Madison, Thomas Jefferson, and James Monroe; and they were damned by two others—George Washington and John Adams. Through Freneau's newspapers, he commented on the major national events and conditions of the decade: the transition from the Washington and Adams administrations to the "Virginia Dynasty," the periodic threats of war with both England and France, the economic instability of the times, the increase in immigration, the gradual extension of the suffrage, and the spread of deism. He tried to alter public reaction to Jay's Treaty with England, to the "X Y Z" affair, and to the Alien and Sedition Acts. In a time when the actions of England and France greatly affected conditions within the United States, Freneau's prose and his poetry, not surprisingly, deal much with these two countries. It was also a

time when many in the United States were looking to other countries for assurance that their experiment in government was the
"coming thing." So Freneau's readers became well acquainted with
the French Revolution and with the various forms of government
adopted by the French; and they followed the trials of Ireland, of
Poland, of Holland, and of Prussia. And the sufferings of the British
under their king were always underscored to reassure American
citizens that their way was right. Both internationally and nationally, the decade was a turbulent one; and Freneau reflected and
sometimes contributed to that turbulence.

The Federalist opinion of Freneau has been the lasting one, and it
has, to a large part, been an obstacle to serious study of his prose.
Freneau's works never sold well in Federalist New England;
Timothy Dwight summarized Connecticut opinion in 1793:
"Freneau, your printer, linguist, &c., is regarded here as a mere
incendiary, or rather as a dispicable tool of bigger incendiaries, and
his paper as a public nuisance."[1] While Washington, in an oft-
quoted phrase, described Freneau as a "rascal," Alexander Hamilton considered Freneau a real threat to order and stability—as "a
man who is continually machinating against the public happiness."[2]
George Gibbs, biographer of the second Secretary of the Treasury,
Oliver Wolcott, described Freneau's paper in this manner: it "was
notorious for its scandalous falsehood and misrepresentation, its
fulsome adoration of Mr. Jefferson, and its gross abuse of leading
federal men."[3] We do not take seriously a writer so described. Too
often we forget the other side—that Jefferson praised Freneau and
his paper for saving the United States' republican form of government. Today, an examination of Freneau's newspapers and essays show that he was far more than a party hack; that he was fairly
moderate; and that, except when his favorite causes were en-
dangered, he was able to observe with wit and humor both sides of a
question.

I   *Freneau's Newspapers*—The Daily Advertiser *(1790–1791)*

In 1790, in New York, Freneau first became connected with
Francis Childs and John Swaine, owners of the *Daily Advertiser*,
and later they became his financial partners in the *National Gazette*.
The nature of Freneau's employment with the *Daily Advertiser* is
uncertain, but the salary was sufficient for Freneau and his new wife
to maintain themselves in New York. Since Freneau was not the

chief editor, we cannot know how much he affected the editorial policy of the paper; and we can only guess his views from those articles and poems which he later reprinted, or from those articles which bear either his initials or a signature which he used again later. His connection with the paper was relatively short. His poems begin appearing in its pages in the spring of 1790; his prose works, possibly, in the middle of June. By February, 1791, he was looking for a change, as is evidenced by his proposals for establishing a Monmouth gazette; by May, he had left New York, even though his poems continued to appear in the *Daily Advertiser* until he had started the *National Gazette*.

Of his identifiable prose and poetry appearing in the *Daily Advertiser*, not many are about controversial topics. His works reflect the debate over a permanent location for the seat of Congress, but even this rather serious controversy he dealt with lightly in "Description of NEW-YORK one-hundred and fifty years hence" and in the poems "Nabby" and "Nanny." In these, he has a housemaid of New York and one of Philadelphia give their own and their mistresses' views about the change: the New Yorker regrets the loss of the excitement; the Philadelphian welcomes the excitement but rues the increase in work.

But in "The American Soldier" (1791), Freneau dealt more directly with partisan political thinking. The veteran of the Revolutionary War is now poor, far from the center of government ("Removed alike from courtly cringing 'squires,/ The great-man's Levee, and the proud man's grin"), and forgotten by it: "She leaves her soldier—famine and a name!" Freneau also struck out against any evidence of courtly manners in "Rules how to compliment great Men in a proper manner," by pointing out that the man in power is "no more than a fellow citizen."[4] On May 27, 1791, he contributed "Lines Occasioned by reading Mr. Paine's Rights of Man." The poem, while celebrating the *Rights of Man*, spends more time in emphasizing over and over the evils of monarchy and in warning the new nation against kingly pretensions: "Be ours the task the ambitious to restrain,/ And this great lesson teach—that kings are vain." All these poems reflect his growing suspicion of the "airs" assumed by Washington's administration.

In "Letter to a newly elected Young Member of the Lower House" (1790), Freneau becomes even more partisan. In advising against pride in office, he introduces the Anti-Federalist tenet of rotation in office, a limitation on reelection: "Do not suffer yourself to be intoxicated with vanity on account of your momèntary exaltation. —*Rotation* is a mortifying consideration, but in that consists the essence of liberty; and it is this which must once more return you to the mass of the people to participate in those burthens which you had a share in imposing." Then in "Occasioned by a Legislation Bill proposing a Taxation upon Newspapers" (1971), Freneau more directly attacks the administration for its pomp. The speaker of the poem declares " '' tis time to tax the News' ":

> "The well-born sort alone, should read the news,
> No common herds should get behind the scene
> To view the movements of the state machine:
> One paper only, filled with courtly stuff,
> One paper, for one country is enough,
> Where incense offered at Pomposo's shrine,
> Shall prove his house-dog and himself divine."

In these contributions, Freneau now begins to sound more like the editor of the *National Gazette* that he was shortly to be.

II *The* National Gazette (*1791–1793*)

Freneau announced the type of paper the *National Gazette* was to be in the first issue, of October 31, 1791. It was to offer the most important foreign news from British, French, and Dutch papers, plus letters from correspondents. Domestic news would be covered by presentation of original documents, Congressional debates, and decisions of the Supreme Court. Contributions were welcome: "The most respectful attention shall be paid to all decent productions of entertainment in prose or verse that may be sent for insertion, as well as to such political essays as have a tendency to promote the general interests of the Union."[5]

In the third issue, on November 7, Freneau explained that "general interests" were "the great principles upon which the American revolution was founded, a faithful adherence to which can alone preserve the blessings of liberty to this extensive empire." There were, of course, those who interpreted the revolutionary principles differently. Freneau quoted the *United States Gazette*'s description of his paper: "The National Gazette is—the vehicle of party spleen and opposition to the great principles of order, virtue and religion." But a defender of Freneau explained away such charges: "Your paper is an enemy to despots, villains and knaves, consequently, they are your adversaries." The truth about Freneau's paper lies somewhere in between: it was a partisan paper, but it was not a splenetic or an anarchic one.

For the greater part of the two years that Freneau edited the *National Gazette,* he kept to the plan announced in the first issue. Unlike many papers of today, he presented original state documents and allowed his readers to examine them for themselves before reading the essays of the controversialists. Although the publication was anti-Federalist, it presented in full Hamilton's yearly reports on the public debt, his important "Report on Manufactures," his "Report on Loans," and several others. Documents presented were not limited to national affairs; the speeches of John Hancock and George Clinton—both good Anti-Federalist governors—to their respective legislatures were given, as well as a speech by the mayor of Paris, several addresses by the king of England to his Parliament, and the constitution of France. If Freneau's readers had limited their reading to these documents only, they would have been well educated politically.

In addition to these documents and the articles from foreign papers, Freneau also clipped articles from domestic daily papers; and he published ones from both Federalist and Republican dailies, although chiefly from Republican ones. His paper was most partisan in the contributions he printed. Letters bearing news from Americans in other states, in London, in Marseilles, in the West Indies were almost totally favorable to his causes. Although the contributed essays on current controversies championed the Anti-Federalists, responses to them were printed so that both sides of the question could be read. There were few editorials as we know them today; unsigned editorial comment was limited to a few lines but was used consistently only late in the second year of publication. As "fillers" Freneau used poetry—his own or others, most of it not on controversial topics; excerpts from standard works by Swift, Samuel Johnson, or Voltaire; or amusing anecdotes.

The *National Gazette,* during its two years of publication, constantly kept three interrelated issues before its public; and rarely was one issue presented without mention of one or the other. The paper opposed England's domination of America in any way, and it favored friendship with France. Nationally, it opposed the schemes and plans of Alexander Hamilton. And, in matters of social and governmental conduct, it opposed any tendency toward monarchical trappings or traits. Hamilton was accused of favoring England and of instituting royal customs in government; England was accused of encouraging trappings of royalty and of abetting Hamilton's financial schemes. The *National Gazette* attacked the English and their adherents in almost every way possible, and it supported France through the wilder days of the Revolution. When news reached America that King Louis had been executed, Freneau, noting that the British court was in mourning for him, added: *"Follies* of this kind might be forgiven to the prejudices of the European, but that the silly American, just emancipated from a tyrant, should join in the whine of condolence, is indeed lamentably absurd and wholly 'out of order.' " And Freneau printed Brackenridge's famous *mot*, "Louis *Capet* has lost his *Caput*," and his comment on it: "From my use of a pun, it may seem that I think lightly of his fate. I certainly do. It affects me no more than the execution of another malefactor."

Much of the controversy stirred by the *National Gazette* resulted from its criticism of George Washington, and much of this criticism had to do with the administration's so-called monarchical trappings. But the criticism was slow to come. On February 23, 1792, Freneau reported on the previous day's celebration of the president's birthday: "the day concluded with every mark of harmony, good order, and undissembled joy." A year later, however, "Valerius" warned against such celebrations; and a correspondent wrote, "the monarchical farce of the birthday was as usual, kept up." The paper associated Washington's habit of holding levees with monarchism; and by January 5, 1793, the comments became pointed. In an article entitled "To the Noblesse and Courtiers of the United States," the writer sarcastically suggested that a poet laureate was wanted by the administration, one who would praise *"levees, drawing-rooms, stately nods instead of shaking hands, titles of office, seclusion from the people, &c."* This attack was a little too pointed for many, and "Mirabeau" felt obliged on February 13 to defend his right to criticize the President. Generally, such criticism of Washington as was found in the pages of the *National Gazette* was rather mild by today's standards. When Washington was directly named, the criticism was couched as warnings and advice: the advice most often given to him was for him to beware of flatterers and of his advisers.

The adviser the *National Gazette* most earnestly wished Washington to ignore was, of course, Alexander Hamilton. As with that of Washington, the criticism of Hamilton began slowly but intensified. His plan for the excise tax was criticized, as were his recommendation for the national bank and his "Report on Manufactures." The real attack on Hamilton began on March 15, 1792, with the beginning of the "Brutus" essays about Hamilton's funding system. Essays attacking the funding system continued as long as the *National Gazette* did. Other controversies periodically took newspaper space from these three major ones, although the essayists usually managed to connect the current controversy with the "sins" of Hamilton, the English, or the monarchists.

The two hottest controversies during the years of the *National Gazette* were the charges against secretary of state Jefferson that were derived from his employment of Freneau as government translator and from the Genet affair. Both subjects, coincidentally, were debated during the summers, when Congress had recessed— almost as if the lack of other news caused these issues to receive more attention than they otherwise would have. On April 23, 1792, Freneau responded to a charge against him: "He must be a venal wretch, indeed, who thinks that because a man holds a lawful office under government, therefore he is obliged to approve and flatter the most arbitrary measures of that government." Thus the charge of Freneau's serving two masters, the government and the opposition to the government, was raised early; but it was not pursued because other news soon displaced it. The attack was renewed at a time when Freneau, at least, was reduced to printing such contributions as a discussion of a clause in the Vacant Lands Act and advice on the rotation of crops.

On July 28, the *National Gazette* reprinted Hamilton's query as to whether Freneau's government salary was paid him for translations "or for *publications*, the design of which is to vilify those to whom the voice of the people has committed the administration of our public affairs." Freneau replied that "the above is beneath a reply," but he added that an impartial editor is far better than one who is a flatterer. For the most part, Freneau left his defense to others, and the controversy soon widened into a discussion of Jefferson's politi-

cal principles. Freneau reprinted from the *American Daily Adver-*
tiser Monroe's "Vindication," but he also reprinted defenses of
Hamilton's stand on the debate. The charges against Jefferson and
Freneau were periodically revived; Freneau defended himself once
more in his paper of October 20, 1792:

The National Gazette is supported, and only supported, by upwards of
thirteen hundred subscriptions from honest and independent citizens of the
United States, through every part of the Union—the end and tendency of
this paper is to countenance the great revolutionary principles of America—
principles that the Editor will adhere to and support, independent of all
influence, in every possible circumstance and situation, and for the dis-
semination of which, or any abuse of which, he considers himself responsible to the public, to whose republican interests he is forever devoted.

Still, the Federalists kept alive the charge that Freneau was only
Jefferson's paid editor.

The second of Freneau's famous newspaper controversies occurred the following summer, again after Congress had recessed—
during the time when many citizens had left Philadelphia for fear of
yellow fever. As with so many issues, Freneau's treatment of the
Genet affair was not impartial, although, as with others, he did
present both sides. Genet, the new French ambassador, arrived in
Philadelphia Thursday, May 16, 1793, after a triumphant journey
from Charleston, and Freneau described him for his Saturday
readers: "We have no doubt but the popular character and engaging
affability of Citizen Genet, will gain him the esteem of the inhabitants of this city and country; and awaken in them sentiments of
gratitude for our generous allies, the defenders of the rights of man
and real friends to America in the dark days of war and desolation."
The *National Gazette* never changed its mind about the worth of
Genet. When Genet came under attack for violating the principles
of Washington's neutrality proclamation about the French Revolution, many essayists appeared in the pages of the *National*
Gazette to defend him. And his defenders remained true even after
John Jay and Rufus King revealed that Genet had threatened, in
defiance of Washington, to appeal to the people to reverse the
policy of neutrality. When Genet protested to the president in a
letter, and when Jefferson replied with a rebuke that such cor-
respondence should be addressed to him as secretary of state, the
defenders became less enthusiastic. Still, Freneau, in an editorial

comment, felt able to reassure the French that "the hearts of *the people*, and *their hands*, if necessary, are with them and their cause."

Freneau did not turn all of his paper over to political controversialists: his readers were informed about subjects other than political ones. That Freneau shared the inquiring and projecting spirit of the Enlightenment is seen from the space he gave to reports of the various philosophical societies and the attention he paid to findings in agriculture—why crop rotation was favored, what to do about the Hessian fly that was attacking wheat. The paper reported with enthusiasm various projects for canal construction, as it did various archaeological discoveries—old bones found, the controversy over the nature of the Indian mounds. For a time, David Rittenhouse, president of the Philadelphia Philosophical Society, presented his meteorological observations to the paper. Articles on Saturn, the formation of mountains, and Captain William Bligh's safe arrival in the West Indies with his cargo of plants also informed the scientific-minded of Freneau's readers.

Freneau's selection of short accounts shows his interest in reform. He strongly favored a patent bill to protect American inventors, editorialized in favor of the arts and artists, discoursed on the need for improvement in the debtors' prison system, and seemingly printed every account he could find of attempts to halt the slave trade and to encourage political rights for Negroes. He reprinted a review of Phillis Wheatley's poems, a review which he probably approved since her poetry was damned in it as being too much in the English style. Freneau's paper was cited by the opposition for encouraging irreligion, but there are few such instances. He did print a notice of the Deist Elihu Palmer's lecture in Philadelphia, and he approved the dissolution of monasteries in France, but there is little else of this nature.

Freneau's unsigned editorial comments are few and far between, especially in the first year when he relied chiefly on signed contributions and articles from other papers. Most of the short unsigned fillers, however, sound unmistakeably like Freneau, as does a comment on the Americans' unnatural love of gold, or this observation, printed in his paper in May, 1792: "From the present degraded state of royalty in Europe, its secret patrons in this country cannot possibly deduce any arguments in favour of American Kings and Princes." The sentiment is his, and so is the style. "Rules for changing a limited Republican Government into an unlimited hereditary one" (July 4, 1792) is a longer piece that is undoubtedly Freneau's. The first eight rules are sarcastic and clear, as is this excerpt from rule five: "As the novelty and bustle of inaugurating the government will for some time keep the public mind in a heedless and unsettled state, let the *Press* during this period be busy in propagating the doctrines of monarchy and aristocracy. For this purpose it will be particularly useful to confound a mobbish democracy with a representative republic, that by exhibiting all the turbulent examples and enormities of the former, an odium may be thrown on the character of the latter." As the rules continue, however, they become essentially short essays protesting the Hamiltonian system of finance. In becoming longer, they lose their strength as satire and sarcasm.

Freneau's prose is best when it allows his indignation and bitterness to show through his philosophic calm, as when he commented in his paper in February, 1793, about the Federalists' use of George Washington: "It is an old trick of designing characters, to cry up a single individual as the life, safety and *sine qua non* of a nation; and by deifying him, to make themselves the real sovereigns over the people." From sections of an essay on Genet, contributed May 22, 1793, by "An Old Soldier" (undoubtedly one of Freneau's pen names), it seems that Freneau is not so good at praising as censuring—his praise is too high flown, too literary, too contrived: "The bosoms of many hundred freemen beat high with affectionate transport, their souls caught the celestial fire of struggling liberty, and in the enthusiasm of emotion, they communicated their feelings to the worthy and amiable representative of the French nation. What a delicious repast for a mind interested in the cause of humanity!" Freneau is best when he speaks simply and ironically.

The *National Gazette,* one of the most controversial newspapers of the time, was also one of the best. When Aaron Burr sent his wife a copy in November, 1791, he told her to give it to a friend but to "take care, however, to get it back and preserve it, as it is one of Freneau's. . . . If you find them amusing, you may command them regularly."[6] This paper is informative and interesting, and it is also illustrative of the controversies and styles of Freneau's time.

III   *The* Jersey Chronicle *(1795–1796)*

In one of Freneau's "Old Soldier" essays published in the *National Gazette* on May 22, 1793, Freneau praises the French and maligns the British; but he adds that "it must not be imagined from what I have said, that my voice is for war. Could we render France any essential assistance, war would be our *duty*, it would be our *security*; but the assistance which we can give her, may be better accomplished in peace." Too often Freneau is pictured as a rabid and radical Francophile who forgot all caution in his advocacy of the French cause. Such lack of moderation would not be in keeping with the ideal of the Enlightenment. Freneau was for republicanism but against mob democracy, even though he may have flattered the mob. In the *Jersey Chronicle*, however, the balance of the *National Gazette* is missing. Where the *National Gazette* allowed space for rebuttal during its controversies, the *Jersey Chronicle* printed very few essays that opposed its editorial stand on its main issue, Jay's Treaty with England. Generally, the *Chronicle* damned the treaty, which did not mention major American complaints about British incitement of Indians, impressment of American seamen, or the touchy question of trade with the West Indies. The only thing the treaty did do, it seemed, was to keep the peace—for a while. We could almost say that Jay's Treaty was the paper's reason for being, since the majority of each issue dealt with it, its reception, and its probable consequences. But Freneau once more enlightened his readers by printing the whole of the treaty.

In the *Chronicle*, a large amount of space is devoted to essays reprinted from other papers, chiefly the *Aurora;* there are very few original contributions. It is probable that Freneau is the author of some of the many essays reprinted from the *Aurora*, especially some of those about Jay's Treaty. Now at home in New Jersey, away from the excitement of the capital, Freneau also found time to rework some of his *Daily Advertiser* sketches and to compose others. In this paper there are fewer articles of the scientific sort, but Freneau does find space for recipes for bread; for extracts on the "saints" of Boston, on Ossian, and on the Shaking Quakers; and for a long essay about the character of the Chinese. Thus there was some light reading that was not devoted to denouncing the treaty with England.

In his statement of purpose in the first issue, however, Freneau did not mention the treaty. His purpose was higher: "At this time, when new Republics are forming and new Empires bursting into birth; when the great family of mankind are evidently making their egress from the dark shadows of despotism which have so long enveloped them, & are assuming a character suitable to the dignity of their species, the Editor seizes the opportunity to *renew* his efforts for contributing, in some small degree, to the general information of his fellow citizens in the present history and politics of the world."[7]

But Freneau did not accent the positive for long. On page seven of that first issue he examined and denied the British charge that the French were in a state of anarchy; then he asked, "but if there hath been really a system of annihilation in Europe, hath not Britain all the credit of it to herself?" In the supplement to the first issue, as if to leave no doubt in his readers' minds where he stood, Freneau issued this warning: "let it never be effaced from your minds, that Great Britain sought to enslave you, that she is the enemy of freedom, that she is at this moment waging a cruel warfare against it, and that no effort of her's will remain untried to exterminate it from the Earth." And, in support of his claims about the evil nature of Great Britain, Freneau presented, in issue after issue, letters from American sea captains telling of British harassments and depredations.

In domestic affairs, however, Freneau's paper is more balanced, for it printed essays praising, as well as those denouncing, the president. And he sounds a note of political moderation in the *Jersey Chronicle* which perhaps had not been needed in the *National Gazette*. Although giving all his support to Edmund Randolph in his argument against the administration (he was dismissed for indiscrete relations with the French minister), Freneau concludes, "when Congress meet, the ex-secretary & others implicated in censure, will undoubtedly be honorably exculpated, or charges of malconduct fully proved against them." In other words, one should leave the decision to the legal body having jurisdiction. The most striking instance of this moderation appears in the issue of December 12 in an unsigned editorial statement. Freneau discusses the accusations on both sides concerning Jay's Treaty, and then addresses his readers: "Fellow citizens, as bodies you mean right on both sides; your hard epithets serve only to inflame each other, to our great political damage. . . . War should be avoided if possible, but Britain appears willing to try our patience thoroughly by her wanton and barbarous provocations. . . . How long we shall bear the unprovoked injuries of Great Britain, without retaliation, we ought to leave with our rulers." If it were not for Freneau's attitude toward Britain, we would find it difficult to believe that this, and other pleas for moderation in the paper, came from Freneau's pen. The *Jersey Chronicle* is enlightening for one studying Freneau; but it lacked the excellence of the *National Gazette* for news and controversy.

IV   The Time Piece, and Literary Companion *(1797–1798)*

Like the *Jersey Chronicle*, the New York *Time Piece* carried Freneau's name for only one year; unlike it, the *Time Piece* changed its nature during that year, possibly because Freneau got a new partner after six months. Although at first the paper was almost a literary gazette, Freneau's statement of purpose in the first issue does not indicate that this paper was to be any different from the others. He says he has undertaken the task because he feels that a periodical "has the fairest chance . . . [to] render man that exalted character, and give him that real pre-eminence which he was evidently designed to hold on the scale of animated nature."[8] Although he continued to print state documents, Freneau now educated his readers more through *belles-lettres* than through politics.

He filled the majority of his pages with poetry, history, light essays, and travelers' accounts. He reprinted his translation of Abbe Robin's *Travels* and his own Tomo Cheeki essays from the *Jersey Chronicle*. There were excerpts from the "best authors," accounts of Napoleon's Italian campaign, and descriptive accounts of towns in Italy. For his poetry section, Freneau was evidently so deluged by poetry of the drearier sort that he tactfully sought after a few issues to direct his contributors to other subjects: "As the genial month of May is now scattering the clouds, and dispensing the blessings of sunshine, it is hoped, we shall be favoured, particularly from the ladies, with poetical communications of a more cheerful and lively nature." The most prolonged controversy in his pages in the early months concerned the state of the New York theater.

By the end of May, however, Freneau had begun to allow current political controversy into his pages. On May 5, 1797, he printed a poem attacking the conservative Philadelphia printer, William Cobbett; and he reprinted, without comment, Jefferson's rash letter to Phillip Mazzei in which he complained about American Anglophiles. But the paper from June to September is so very uneven, that we have the impression that Freneau and his partner Alexander Menut could not quite decide what to do with it. There is much concern with the rising desire for war against France, especially in Freneau's "Sketches on Different Subjects." In them, after a description of ancient and modern kings, he defines navies as existing only to take care of the overflow of nobility for insular governments; and he scorns the American navy then being built. Freneau fears it is intended for use against France, and he issues a warning to those so intending: "when the people of America are wise enough to see that war is hatching only for the benefit of comparatively few individuals, they will be cautious of listening to men who are artfully endeavoring to draw them into a snare that has produced the misery of all nations, and made the world a slaughter house, or, almost literally, a den of thieves and robbers." Freneau also began once more to protest the government's fiscal policies; this time he wrote as "Mat. Moonshine, junior," a rough countryman, to whom it makes sense to pay off the country's debt only by breeding pigs.

As part of the change in the *Time Piece*, Freneau indulged in controversy with John Fenno, his old rival of the *United States Gazette*, and with William Cobbett. He advised them that they should not be so frivolous when the yellow fever was again attacking Philadelphia, and he noted Fenno's misquotation of an article in the *Time Piece*: "and yet if fame does not greatly wrong him *political honesty* is a science with which he has yet to form some acquaintance." Freneau, who quoted Cobbett as saying he had been plagued by the *Time Piece*, responded: "it has also been a plague to some others of his brethren, and will go on to be so, till they are hustled into their native dog-kennels." Then he printed his poem, "To Peter Porcupine":

> From Penn's famous city what hosts have departed,
> The streets and the houses are nearly deserted,
> But still there remain
> Two Vipers, that's plain,
> Who soon, it is thought, yellow flag will display;
> Old Porcupine preaching,
> And Fenno beseeching
> Some dung-cart to wheel him away.

Through the years, Freneau had not grown more delicate in his language of controversy.

The stronger tone of the *Time Piece* was possibly displeasing to Freneau's partner, for notice was given on September 13, 1797, that their partnership was dissolved. Henceforth Freneau was to be allied with M.L. Davis, the future biographer of Aaron Burr and his political lieutenant; and the style of the paper was to be changed to "make room for a greater variety of the current news of the times, and such original communications as may be had from able pens among ourselves." As Freneau had done in previous papers, he now continued to link together aristocratic leanings, the Federalists, and the British. The new partners enlist their readers' sympathies against the British by telling them that it was a British ship which had brought the yellow fever to the United States that fall; by recalling for them that November 25 was the anniversary of the evacuation of New York by the British, and by telling them that only when Britain was peaceful would America forget those wrongs done to her.

Actually, despite the new partners' promises, the paper did not carry many contributed essays about current controversies. There were, however, more original contributions by Freneau—some fanciful, some serious. One article, written from the point of view of "u," "g," and "h," was addressed to the American printers "who, no doubt, think the new fangled spelling very neat and fashionable, and besides lay their account in finding at the year's end a considerable diminution of expense in the article of types." Equally light is "Ridiculous Distress of a Country Weekly News Printer." Because of rains, the printer's exchange newspapers failed to arrive, and so, with the aid of a traveler, guessing at foreign news, he composed his paper anyway: *The whole from being a number of hearsays, rumours, and reports, was the mere shadow of news: but still it was a newspaper; and gave great and general satisfaction!!!* On October 16, Freneau began printing "The Book of Odes," which dealt satirically with current conditions; and the "Hezekiah Salem" essays began on October 23.

Of more serious nature was a series of three essays by Freneau signed "A.B." and entitled "On Imprisonment for Debt." The first is of uneven quality, and in it Freneau tries to trace the philosophical and legal origins of imprisonment for debt. The second essay is stronger, as it departs from philosophical questing. Freneau suggests that benevolent societies be formed to alleviate the miseries of the imprisoned debtor's family, and he also proposes that the debtors be put to work since idleness leads to wickedness: "Where is there an instance of a person shut up in jail for one, two, three or more years, that did not come out a worse character than he went in." In the final essay, he suggests a plan to introduce trades in jails and to sell the resultant work at a low price in shops, thus enabling those imprisoned to work themselves out of debt. Freneau had long protested against debtors' prisons, but this series contains his most coherent statement on the subject.

Freneau himself came close to being imprisoned for debt in New York this winter, but he somehow escaped and joined his brother in Charleston. On March 19, 1798, shortly after his return, the *Time Piece* announced that the business in the future would be conducted by the firm of M. L. Davis & Co. Thus Freneau finally disassociated himself from a venture which began much like a general interest magazine but which was transformed into a party newspaper. The paper was never very successful, and Freneau was probably never very happy with it.

V *Essay Series*

Throughout his journalism career, Freneau took advantage of the easily available newspaper space to present essays on different subjects. His best are those signed by one of his created characters—characters who allow Freneau to pose as a detached observer of society, or as one who is all too attached to it but who sees it from a different viewpoint than his own. He started this type of essay in the *Freeman's Journal* with his "Pilgrim" series, and he continued it in his *Miscellaneous Works* with the character now named "The Philosopher of the Forest." In the *Daily Advertiser*, the character became Opay Mico, a visitor from another culture, and he became Tomo Cheeki in Freneau's *Jersey Chronicle* and *Time Piece*. Freneau created Hezekiah Salem for the *Time Piece*, and he resurrected Robert Slender (who had also appeared in the *Miscellaneous Works*) for a series in the *Aurora* in 1800. The quality of these essays is uneven, for Freneau is not so good when talking the elevated language of the philosopher as he is when he writes as the common man on topics of current interest. The Pilgrim, the Philosopher, Tomo Cheeki—all are inferior to Robert Slender.

Despite the weakness of some of the "Pilgrim" essays, the character does give Freneau a wide scope in his compositions; for, since the Pilgrim has traveled the world widely, he can discuss comparative manners and morals. He has lived long, so he can offer sage advice. He lives in the country, and thus can comment on the virtues of a rural life; but he is not far from Philadelphia, and therefore can offer detached observations on the fads and fashions of town life. Freneau achieves even more flexibility by making the Pilgrim an advice-giving columnist. Thus, without excessive manipulation, Freneau can have the Pilgrim talk on any subject by simply composing a letter to him—and some of the letters are better creations than the answers.

Unfortunately, the Pilgrim (or Freneau) all too often believes that the elevated style is best, as in this example from the Pilgrim's musings on the Christmas season: "Amidst this melancholy scene, so congenial to my feelings, amid these clouds, these snows, these leafless trees, that afford us the liveliest emblematic views of the vanity of life; when the birds have ceased their notes, when the quadrupeds of the wood have shrunk into their dens to wait the return of the spring, is it becoming that the human race alone, who are brought into the world naturally more helpless than the meanest of the brute creation, should give themselves up to riot and drunkenness?"[9] This style is not consistently used, but Freneau returns to it all too often.

In this first series, Freneau was, however, developing ideas of a style proper for an American public. On January 30, 1782, he chides "Bryan O'Krazie," an Irish preacher, for using Latin and elegant verse in his sermons to a backwoods audience: "adapt your discourses to the plain understandings, and even to the ignorance of the generality of those who are to hear you, and I think a parish will soon be at your service." In concluding his letter of advice, the Pilgrim shows himself firmly a member of the Enlightenment: "Let what you say be your own, and convince the world that God has given you and every man among the moderns an originality of reason and understanding, as well as to the moralists, poets, and philosophers of antiquity."

The passages of the Pilgrim's that are the most vigorous are on subjects which Freneau feels most strongly about, as when he insists on January 2, 1782, that England is the cruelest nation: "After a criminal is suspended to a gibbet, no nation but this takes him down when but half dead, rips up his bowels, tears out his heart, and throws it reeking with blood into his face!" But even without a sensational subject, the Pilgrim can be direct, as when he discusses that Jeffersonian ideal, agrarianism:

If a man can be said to possess an independent fortune, it is he whose industry draws immediately from the earth the necessary supports of life.

None need be poor where there is plenty of lands, and where people are suffered to purchase at a reasonable rate, and can say, "This is our own." Health, cheerfulness, and a contented mind, are the natural attendants on a rural life; and if there remain on this earth any traces or resemblances of the first paradise, they existed among the forests, mountains, and vallies of this western world.

Such philosophizing seems much more genuine, less latinate, less trite, than the Pilgrim's musings on Christmas.

Of the Pilgrim's contributions, one of the most interesting consists of letters from four correspondents and the Pilgrim's responses to them—all printed January 16, 1782. The first is from "Eliakim Stout, Koachman to Mrs. Margery Fidget," which, as the Pilgrim says, "I shall give it precisely as it was sent to me, that his ideas may not suffer any alteration by being wrought into a more elaborate diction":

but ever since we have been in this toun, my mistrus has spent the evaning out, and she stais there sum times til five o'klok in the morning; and it maks no ods to her what sort of wether it is, because she sits in the hous by the fier, but I and the horses stay in the rane; and I wunders how the poor things keeps so fat, for I cant, and I eats hearty too; if their skins didnt turn the rane beter than my koat, I am shure they would katch kold, and bark like our *Watch*, as I do; but then I feeds 'em and rules 'em well; aie, I wish my mistrus would tak as much kare of me, as I dos of them.

Freneau's experiment in the dialect of the uneducated is, unfortunately for this series, only an experiment.

In the second letter, "Rachel Sleepless," a young girl from the country who is now a housemaid, phrases her complaint this way: "I hope you will advise people of note to fall upon some other methods of living that their domestics may enjoy some little satisfaction in life, as well as themselves." While both servants express approximately the same sentiments, the first letter, being more natural, makes its point better. The third letter has "Maria Flutter" plead, "do, sir, say something in favour of plays. The young people of the city are really tired of their lives for want of some such entertainment now and then in the winter evenings." Here, as with the coachman, Freneau has caught the style and the sentiment of his character fairly accurately. The last letter is from "Timothy Legible," a book salesman who is indignant that he is not offered more for his wares: "The other day I was offered four and six pence for Locke upon Human Understanding, and two dollars for Shakespear's works compleat." These correspondents, despite their stock names, have credible complaints. For each correspondent, the Pilgrim composes a solution. He advises Mrs. Margery Fidget to keep earlier hours, and for the people she visits to keep sheds for visiting horses and the kitchen for the coachmen; Rachel is advised to return to the country where earlier hours are kept; he forbids plays to Maria until she can "convince her friends that she returns from that species of diversion better and wiser than she went." As for the bookseller, the Pilgrim offers little hope—he must "exchange his books for commodities in more demand, viz. a few casks of sugar, indigo, hides, tallow, soap, candles, &c. &c." The whole series is done in a light manner: although Freneau is intent on lecturing his audience, the letter-answer device enables him to do so in an entertaining, albeit nonphilosophical, manner.

For *Miscellaneous Works* (1788), his first published volume containing prose, Freneau gathered together many of his essays from the *Freeman's Journal*—some he rewrote; others he rearranged. He took six of the "Pilgrim" essays, added five others, and formed a series under the pen name of the "Philosopher of the Forest." In his rearrangement, most of the essays now bear the same level of seriousness and the same philosophical tone. The character is the same as the Pilgrim; in fact, the Philosopher introduces himself as such: "I have now spent upwards of thirty years wandering up and down the world as a pilgrim; a line of life which I can assure you, has, like all others, its hardships, discouragements and difficulties, as well as its pleasures and advantages."[10] The Philosopher is, however, more given to discuss general tendencies than was the Pilgrim. Through him, Freneau discusses the nature of man. In essays two and three, Freneau reworks the creation myth. Firando, Nature's journeyman, endows all animals, including man, with virtue. But, on returning from a brief absence, Firando discovers his inept colleagues have created discord, symbolized by the rattlesnake. All Firando can do to correct the situation is to give the snake rattles. Thus man, originally virtuous, must live with discord; or, as the Philosopher expresses it in a later essay, "discord and disorder are interwoven with the nature and constitution of the human race."

There is, however, some relief to this gloomy picture. The fourth essay describes the country parson who lives near by, and it praises him for being humble and happy in his rustic surroundings: Freneau always praised the idyllic country life. Despite some present evils, typified by the Indians' being dispossessed of their lands, the Philosopher sees a greater future: "It is not easy to conceive what will be the greatness and importance of North America in a century or two to come, if the present fabric of Nature is upheld, and the people retain those bold and manly sentiments of freedom, which actuate them at this day." Man is vicious now, but the future holds hope.

A few essays are satirical, but Freneau works to make them consistent with the Philosopher's character. Number five, "Containing some *particulars relative* to the Island of SNATCHAWAY," criticizes Great Britain, but the Philosopher, in a headnote, softens the criticism: "At the same time that we delineate the vices and follies of this Island, let us not forget, that she is a friend to science; maintains a bold, warlike, and enterprising race of men; and may justly boast of having produced a considerable number of persons, whose actions and sentiments have done real honour to the nature of man."

The wrongs of England presented in the essay, however, are those Freneau was to constantly argue: there is much talk of liberty but little in fact exists. The people are allowed to complain; but, "in return for this glorious privilege, the people at large are the slaves of the rich and great; are saddled with kings, royal families, lords spiritual and temporal, and myriads of their needy dependents." In this essay, Freneau also shows his championship of France: "The people of Fickle-land, on the opposite coast of the continent, although, perhaps, the most civilized, brave, generous and humane in the world, are the perpetual objects of their abuse and ridicule."

Number nine, also somewhat satirical, deals with the United States by having a Polish visitor converse with the clergyman and the Philosopher. The traveler, who had expected to find all good in America, voices his dissatisfaction with it. The clergyman reminds the traveler that he should not have expected felicity on this earth, but the Philosopher disagrees—felicity is only to be apprehended through man's senses and through examples in this real world. The essay is well organized, for it gives Freneau, through the traveler, an opportunity to chide Americans for their pettiness, and, through the Philosopher and clergyman, a chance to discuss the more abstract problem of good and evil. The essay is a good blend of the abstract and concrete.

For more relaxed discussions of mundane matters, Freneau used Robert Slender, the weaver in the poem "A Journey from Philadelphia to New-York." After a preliminary "Advice to Authors" and "Robert Slender's Idea of the Human Soul," the Slender essays are divided into two sections: "Tracts and Essays on Several Subjects" and "Essays, Tales, and Poems." In "Advice to Authors," we are told that Slender is a weaver, a traveler, and an author: "Writing and weaving seem to have been rather his amusements than his serious occupations; and one proof of his having been a man of sense is, his not having depended upon authorship alone for a subsistence." Thus Slender is an independent craftsman, and his independence enables him to wander at will, to observe what he finds interesting, to travel when and where he feels like it. While Freneau could not endow Slender with much classical learning, he did give him an inquiring mind and common sense. He is not rich, but neither is he excessively poor; he is one of the ruled, not a ruler. He is, as Freneau would proudly claim him to be later, "One of the Swinish Multitude"—and thus he is one of the very few spokesmen for this class in the American literature of Freneau's lifetime.

The Slender of *Miscellaneous Works* likes to form rules and to dispense advice, and his rules in "Advice to Authors" make sense in an amusing way. He warns against dedicatory epistles and against scholars, for "a mere scholar and an original author are two animals as different from each other as a fresh and salt water sailor." Many of the rules deal with handling poverty with equanimity, on the assumption that to be an author is to be poor. Slender concludes that, if Fortune is fickle, one should not fall into bad habits "but retire to some uninhabited island or desert, and there, at your leisure, end your life with decency." Slender's "Directions for Courtship" are the same mixture of sense and nonsense. One is never to write to a loved one, and never to talk geography to her. Above all, one never refers to any portion of the anatomy—a rule which enables Freneau to satirize some of the euphemisms of his day.

Slender confidently advises authors and lovers; he also gives "Rules and Directions how to Avoid Creditors, Sheriffs, Constables, &c." After a beginning premise that "there is certainly no moral evil in the mere circumstance of being in debt," twelve rules follow. (1) Know the streets and geography of Philadelphia well. (2) Leave one's usual dwelling place. (3) Do not mingle with one's neighbors. (4) Appear only in fogs or at night. (5) Make sure the coast is clear before appearing. (6) Keep in mind always what one's creditors look like. (7) One shouldn't worry if one meets a creditor who is a philosopher, a mathematician, or a politician—he won't see one. (8) If one does meet a creditor, one should know something with which one can flatter his ego, so he will forget the debt. (9) If one is small, one should keep behind someone taller. (10) One should not carry a lantern at night. (11) One is not even safe on Sunday; someone may track one home. (12) If caught, one should have a letter prepared saying that one has just inherited an estate. Debtors and debtors' prisons were always one of Freneau's causes, but only as Slender does he discuss them so lightheartedly.

Slender is also a philosopher, but one who explains himself with everyday examples. In his "Idea of the Human Soul," he posits that man is "still sustained in the necessary perfection by the wisdom of the deity"; but, when accounting for different personalities, he compares men to water with different alcoholic spirits added. The analogy bemuses him, and he contemplates enthusiastically the addition of American whiskey: "we are carried beyond ourselves into those joyous regions where the first source of generosity, bravery, benevolence and good-nature is displayed to our enraptured view." It is typical that Slender talks more confidently of the effects of whiskey than of the origins of the soul.

Slender, a good observer, is good at characterizations. An old bachelor is "the most selfish of all human beings," and a tutor is "an animal that would be truly worthy of pity, if there were any reason to believe that he himself was at all sensible of the misery of his condition." A series of short essays describing men of varied fortune as seen on the streets of Philadelphia is especially good. "The Market Man" on his way to market is gloomy but pleased on his return; "The Man in Business" pays attention to nothing as he walks, and he "is little better than a perambulating machine, till he comes to the scene of action, his counting house, or his law shop." In contrast, "The Man out of Business" walks slowly, looks about him, and his talk "most commonly turns upon the scarcity of money or the peculiar and unparalleled poverty and rascality of the present age." When Slender describes "The Debtor," he shifts to first person. He, as a debtor, avoids creditors, shivers a lot when he sees them, "and it is only at church, on Sundays, that I can look one or more of them in the face with any tolerable degree of composure."

In "The City Poet," we expect Freneau to vent his spleen about the frustrations of publishing poetry; but Slender's attitudes and viewpoints are maintained. The essay gives the meeting between Slender and Menalcas, the poet, who raves about the country life: " 'Here the inhabitants are innocent and happy, and, in my opinion, bear some considerable resemblance, in their manners, to the ancient people of the golden age.' " Freneau the poet has several poems which claim the same thing; but Freneau the essayist is now writing, and his creation, Slender, responds: " 'STRANGE, thought I, that the man can be so entirely ignorant of the world as to imagine, that the distance of little more than half a mile from the city can produce such a change in himself as well as in the morals of the people: he must, no doubt be poetically mad!' " This is what makes Freneau so enjoyable and interesting—his ability to mock himself. But Freneau is not done with poets yet, for the group criticizes Menalcas for attempting a biblical epic, and Slender cautions him: " 'If poetry, as being the language of exalted passion, has its peculiar charms and captivating beauties for some minds, we ought still to remember that prose is the language of sober reason, and therefore of infinitely more use in the affairs, and for the amusement of the generality of mankind, than the other' " This is not only the rationalist Freneau speaking but also the democratic Freneau who had in mind service to other men.

Of the first series of Slender's essays, "The Splenetic Indian" is perhaps the most uneven, for Freneau is again poking fun at one of his cherished poetic ideas—the concept of the Noble Savage. But Freneau cannot entirely deny the concept, and so the essay points in many different directions and achieves many different moods. Slender, escorted to an Indian village by Tomo-cheeki, welcomes the experience, for "I thought myself happy that I had been permitted to come into the world in an age when some vestiges of the primitive men and their manner of living were yet to be found." The Indian, Tomo-cheeki, too, fears the vanishing of his race—he had a dream in which his ancestors appeared: *Brother, it is time thou hadst also arrived in our abodes: thy nation is extirpated, thy lands are gone, thy choicest warriors are slain; the very wigwam in which thou residest is mortgaged for three barrels of hard cider!*

With the exception of the last clause, the speech is in keeping with Romantic mournfulness, which is furthered by Slender's comment as they arrive at the Indian village: "The situation was highly romantic, and of that kind which naturally inclines one to melancholy." But the tone soon shifts. Tomo-cheeki, recalling that he has signed his lands away, contemplates suicide, asserting that there is nothing new under the sun. But a French trader appears and offers brandy in exchange for beaver skins. This, Tomo-cheeki decides after tasting the brandy, is something new: "I have now learned wisdom, and am convinced that it is VARIETY *alone that can make life desireable.*" And suddenly, a new, unlooked-for moral has been introduced. The mixture in this essay of the realistic portrayal of the Indian and the Romantic view of him demonstrates the mixture in Freneau of hard-headed rationality and some dissatisfaction with this attitude.

This same mixture also appears in one of the more interesting selections in the second series of Robert Slender's essays, "Light Summer Reading." The placement of this essay under Slender's name, plus the headnote (*"Which may possibly please such as have a true taste for modern Novels"*) leads us to suspect that Freneau is attempting to satirize the sentimental novel. But this essay also suffers from Freneau's mixture of satiric and serious treatment. The plot, if such it is, shows a visitor to Bermuda being told of Marcia, whose dominant trait is melancholy. She is pining away for a student who impressed her and then sailed away. The visitor and his guide encounter a poet who sends her verses—some of the local inhabitants think these verses help to make her mad. Later, the two discover Marcia has died and pass by her funeral. While the officiating clergyman goes back for his forgotten book, an Indian addresses the mourners on the subject of death; but he is accused of heresy by the clergyman on his return. This very slender plot line gives Freneau the opportunity to discuss melancholy, poetry, and the afterlife. Some of the discussion is in fun; some, seriously done.

"Light Summer Reading" often seems mockingly autobiographical. Thrown in apparently gratuitously is the information that Marcia has a canary and has received a poem asking her to release it. Now in 1778, Freneau had composed "On Amanda's Singing Bird," with these lines, phrased by the canary: "Dear Amanda!—leave me free,/ And my notes will sweeter be;/ On your breast, or in the tree!"

This poetic mockery continues as Slender quotes "To Marcia," which describes the girl listening to the poet:

> She sate, regardless of my art,
> And counted seconds by the clock:
> *And thus*, she cry'd, *shall verse decay;*
> *And thus the world shall pass away!*

An aspiring poet would not find Marcia's reaction very complimentary. The last line of another poem included in "Light Summer Reading" is one which Freneau later reworked for the more famous "The Wild Honeysuckle." In its original form, the line appears as follows:

> So drooping hangs the fading rose,
> When summer sends the driving shower,
> So to the grave *Marcella* goes,
> Her whole duration but an hour.

Marcia finally died, we are told, after reading a similar poem about the misery of man, the brevity and infelicity of life, and the certainty of death. Although Freneau wrote several poems of this type, the spokesman in the essay deplores the reading of such works by the young. "Light Summer Reading," while faulty, is intriguing because Freneau mocks his own poetic ideas and attitudes.

The other longer selection of Slender's second series, "The Voyage of Timberoo-Tabo-Eede, an Otaheite Indian," is more consistent but also more derivative. A three-part account, the first gives instructions from the king of the island to his explorers which order them to sail to the East and to take possession of all countries they find, to conduct themselves according to their own customs; to extort necessary food by capturing or killing the native prince, and to take along a priest to keep them faithful. The second part is the journal kept by Timberoo of the voyage. He describes the intense cold, then the first inhabited town, where the language "seemed *barbarous* in a high degree, as being *very unlike our own*." Timberoo spends much time describing the land's religion, but he does not think much of it: "it is high time for some benevolent divinity to descend upon the island a second time, as it is at present overrun with every species of wickedness." The third section is shortest—a

State Paper of Otaheite that concludes that a conquest of such a land would not be worth the effort. Freneau's premise—having a barbarian set out to civilize the world—is good; but, once Timberoo arrives in the civilized land, Freneau abandons most of the attempt to maintain the fiction; and the middle section devolves into cynical observations that are not necessarily consistent with Freneau's barbaric traveler.

The remaining Slender essays in *Miscellaneous Works* are more lighthearted. "The Power of Novelty" begins philosophically with the statement of Nature's bounteous variety, but it soon becomes more concrete with the specific complaint of a newspaper editor who feels the need to season his paper with various disasters, "but peace has ruined everything." In "The Sick Author," Slender visits the writer in his garret. The author, in delirium, tells of his former lives—now he is "doing penance in the character of an American poet." Typical of Slender (if somewhat reminiscent of Swift) is "The Academy of Death. A Fragment," in which Slender dreams he visits that illustrious Academy where are lodged all the great sages of antiquity. He, as a lowly weaver, is about to be shooed away by Death, but is granted time to question some of the guests—a device which gives Freneau a chance to speculate about the looks and manners of his favorite authors. Among other information, Slender is told by Homer that Ulysses stayed so long from Ithaca because Penelope was a jilt and a shrew. The dream breaks off just when, we suspect, Freneau's invention ran out. Immediately following, and perhaps meant to be a companion piece, is "Robert Slender's Idea of a Visit to a Modern Great Man." In it, the emphasis is on the fact that Slender, a weaver and a tradesman, does not need to be, and is not, treated with good manners by his "betters." While Slender often wanders off into uncharacteristic subjects, Freneau never lets us forget that he is one of the common people. Of the two major spokesmen of *Miscellaneous Works*, Slender is the more original and more likeable character.

To the Philosopher of the Forest, Freneau gave those essays written in the character of moralist, traveler, and sage; the majority of the rest he ascribed to Robert Slender. But Freneau could attribute to neither character a few of the essays, which include an exchange between Christopher Clodhopper and Priscilla Tripstreet on extravagances, a dissertation on "esquire," a complaint about "little" men called "The Picture Gallery," Adam Blackbeard's "A

Discourse upon Beards," and "The Antiquarian," a discourse against too-great pride in mere book learning. The subject matter of this variety ranges from the minuscule to the profound; the tone, from light pleasantry to heavy sarcasm.

Among the better essays in this group is "The Sailor's Relief," in which an innkeeper proposes that a ship be built on dry land for the relief of out-of-work sailors. Freneau uses the hoary device of an innkeeper's producing a sailor's manuscript left behind in lieu of payment. But the manuscript is short, and it is recorded, as the innkeeper assures us, in the sailor's own dreadful language. Once more Freneau writes in dialect: "At 12 last night, fell in with a watchman, the new building then bearing due west, and Christ church steeple nearly fourth east. As bad luck would have it he carried no lanthorns, so that he suddenly boarded me in the dark, and at the first shock carried away all the breast hooks of my new blue jacket, the starboard lifts of my half worn castor hat, and nearly two thirds of the after leech of my old great coat."

When we turn from this frivolity to an essay like "On City Burying Places," we find an entirely different Freneau. In this work in which he protests against burials in churches and within city limits, he responds to the defense that, in churches, the dead remind us of our mortality: "But to be put in mind of *death* and *sleep* at the same time is rather overdoing the matter; for I must confess that most of our pulpit orators display so little of oratorial gesture in their persons, and so little of energetic eloquence in their discourses, that between the *dead* men that surround us in the adjacent graves, and the *living* man in the pulpit, I most frequently return drowsy, discontented and melancholy from a place where I vainly hoped to have my spirits raised." Although making a serious point, Freneau still seeks to leaven the matter with wit.

The prose of *Miscellaneous Works* often reveals Freneau's faults as a prose stylist. Too many of the essays are unfocused because they lack a singleness of purpose. This fault is, perhaps, one of enthusiasm—Freneau wants to comment on too many things in each essay. But the "Philosopher of the Forest" series is more consistent in tone than the "Pilgrim" series in the *Freeman's Journal*, and the character of Robert Slender remains fairly consistent. The essays in *Miscellaneous Works* are essentially revisions of first attempts; the ideas and the originality are here, but Freneau later achieved greater skill in producing a consistent series of essays.

The series of which Tomo-Cheeki is the spokesman was written over almost a decade: Freneau used essays previously published in the *Daily Advertiser* (August–September, 1790) and added original ones to form the series in the *Jersey Chronicle* (May–October, 1795). This series he in turn revised, reordered, and extended to form the final series of the *Time Piece*. These essays return to the well-used device of a traveler's giving his impressions of his first visit to "civilization." But instead of using his commentator as a chiefly satirical device, Freneau uses Tomo-Cheeki as a Noble Savage. Thus he is a traveler who, while expressing his amazement at the white man's ways, also gives the reader his own positive values that are derived from the way of Nature and Reason. In these essays, therefore, we find again the Pilgrim and the Philosopher of the Forest; but he appears this time in Indian regalia.

Our introduction to this philosophical Indian comes because, again, his landlord has discovered a manuscript which Tomo-Cheeki has left behind. The landlord describes his guest as grave and melancholy: "While his fellow deputies were carousing in taverns and dram shops, he would walk into the fields and woods."[11] The first essay in the manuscript gives initial impressions—the cobblestones hurt Tomo-Cheeki's feet; and all the faces he sees are discontented because the people have "turned aside from the walks of nature." The second essay gives his description of what the "walks of nature" are. In the savage life, all wants are satisfied by nature. There is no private property, no taxes, no jealousy, no fear: "We are carried along upon the great wheel of things. We trouble ourselves not about the uncertainties, or the seeming irregularities of its motions. When the comet extends its long glittering tail over our thick forests, or when the moon puts on her black mantle of mourning, we apprehend no cause of alarm. It is the work of the great spirit of the universe, who sleepeth not, but day and night guides his wonderful machine in the way that is best." Tomo-Cheeki is an amazingly Enlightened Indian, for in speaking of the universe as a machine, he echoes Isaac Newton.

He also follows the thinkers of the Enlightenment in speculating about the reasons for man's leaving this golden state of nature. Tomo-Cheeki asserts that originally there was perfect equality, but man has now become "a mean, base, cruel and treacherous being." The reason for this change is social organization: "It is from false forms of government that the far greater part of human miseries and human vices are derived." In the tenth essay, Tomo-Cheeki repeats this thesis and elaborates on it. Social organization leads men to be miserable by making them want too much. To Tomo-Cheeki, the solution is easy: "Instead then, of contriving thousands of wants, why is it not the first care of legislators to diminish these wants to a very few in number?—Let the head men begin with shewing the simple people that they may be satisfied with three or four enjoyments, and the people will soon follow in their path." This statement is about as political as Tomo-Cheeki ever gets, and he soon returns to his more positive position of the goodness of nature.

While philosophically accepting the idea that each race, including that of the Indian, must end to make way for a better man, Tomo-Cheeki still mourns the Indian's fate. In one essay, Freneau protests expeditions against the Indian as being against the law of Nature: "Why then would you anticipate her designs, and by every means in your power hurry us in a moment from this earth, before nature has said, *There is an end to the children of the forest?*" Tomo-Cheeki declares that armies are sent by the whites "to propagate a principle as disgraceful to your pretended age of philosophy, as it is repugnant to truth and reason, *that the rights of an Indian are not the rights of a man!*" The concluding essay reinforces this theme. In a letter, Tomo-Cheeki compares the white and Indian races to big ships and weeds which are on or in the same stream. The one should not seek to destroy the other, since both are subject to the river's power, which may destroy them both. As in this essay, Tomo-Cheeki is always reasonable, sane, and Enlightened. He does not, however, have the sense of humor of Robert Slender: we are not comfortable with Tomo-Cheeki, whereas we relax with Slender.

The essay series signed by Hezekiah Salem is the shortest and most frivolous. Beginning in the *Time Piece* on October 23, 1797, the seven essays of this group are scattered irregularly through the papers. The individual parts of the series should not even be considered to be essays, for they are really sketches that display Salem's eccentric personality. Through Hezekiah Salem, Freneau takes the opportunity to poke fun at the New Englander, thus anticipating the satire of Washington Irving and James Fenimore Cooper. Salem, the son of a weaver, has been a minister who once considered teaching psalmody as a profession, an ex-whaler, and a pumpkin lover. But Salem is more than a vehicle for caricaturing the New

Englander. Like Slender, he is one of the common people; in fact, he constantly stresses that he is a "little" man. Sly, cunning, and somewhat cowardly, he lives by his wits and by his skill at handicrafts.

The first two sketches establish the character of Hezekiah Salem as a typical New Englander. Nothing does this better, Freneau seems convinced, than a description of his love of pumpkins. Salem declares that the best pumpkins, like the best poets, grow in New England—and that this fact is not to be attributed to coincidence, for pumpkins are the source of inspiration for the New Englander: "When he sits down in his easy chair to reflect soberly and sedately, a pumpkin is the first object that strikes his attention."[12] Salem continues his discussion of the pumpkin in the second sketch, since, "in verity it may be said, this is a subject that cannot easily be exhausted." Irving, later, also described geographical regions by their produce.

Salem, who at one time shared the religious fervor of New England, had been a minister for twenty-five years before he was forced to leave his post after a deacon of his church had discovered him playing ninepins on the bowling green—an entertainment unworthy of his calling. Salem accepted the action that threw him "from the *more elevated* part of mankind to a situation among *the low and simple*"; packed a canoe with his possessions, "consisting of a dog, a cat, a chest of old sermons and other writings, &c., seven pumpkins of the best and largest kind, a hoe, a spade, a straw bed, and some apparel of coarse sort and quality"; and made his way to Long Island. There, after a stint at whaling, he settled down to make baskets which he sent to New York, sending with them his articles to the *Time Piece*. Given this intellectual, traveling background, we fear that Salem will become another Philosopher of the Forest or Pilgrim, but Freneau does not allow Salem to have serious speculation.

Three of the sketches emphasize Salem's smallness, and they show him giving advice to other small men about how to compensate for their stature. In "Rules how to get through a crowd," perhaps the best of the series, he complains of the effort it takes to see anything in a crowd. After getting knocks and bruises by trying to force his way through, Salem finally hit on the most effective method: "Smoking in a crowd, together with a strong breath of garlic, soon procures to a man, a little vacant circle, wherein he may stand at his ease, and as he advances, he remaineth still the centre of the circle." In "A Few Words on Duelling," Salem stresses the contrast between his size and that of his challenger, "Benjamin Bigbones, a man of huge stature and forbidding countenance." In "A Scrap, from a Keg, of Hezekiah Salem's Sermons," in which Salem addresses little men directly, he tells them that they are short only by comparison with others, that their very smallness gives them advantages in moving around more easily. If their soul is great, so are they.

The most philosophical Salem becomes is in "From Hezekiah Salem's Last Basket," in which he gives rules for maintaining a philosophical atmosphere. One must keep the cleaning woman out of the study, must have on hand a generous supply of pumpkin beer, and should live in a "howling" house: "where sitting pensively in a long winter evening, when the wind is to the eastward, and clouds impending, a melancholy sort of music plays through the eaves, and awakens the mind to contemplation." Salem charitably gives rules for achieving such a house, the chief of which is to neglect one's business, and thus one's house. Despite his eccentricities, which provide the reader with amusement, Salem remains a literary device for light mockery rather than a character who can be clearly visualized.

VI   Letters on Various Interesting and Important Subjects

The *Letters* of Robert Slender, published first in the *Aurora*, then as a pamphlet in December, 1799, are essentially political propaganda; but they include some of Freneau's best prose. Much of their content is ephemeral: they talk of the contest for Pennsylvania governor between the Federalist James Ross and the Republican Thomas McKean, the Alien and Sedition Acts and trials, the John Adams administration's policy for Santo Domingo, and the case of the impressed sailor-mutineer Jonathan Robbins. Although the specific topics may be ephemeral, the attitudes and chief character are lasting. Naive Robert Slender has to have complex matters explained to him, but he is a devastating logician who reasons from the tenets he holds. His common sense triumphs over the more educated, sophisticated minds—the lowly and honest triumph over the rich and hypocritical. In these *Letters*, Freneau uses a variety of devices to keep the reader's interest. Whereas earlier series consisted of a diary, in which impressions were recorded, or missives from a relatively stationary recluse, the spokesman in this series moves among a variety of men, argues with them, is frightened by them, and discusses the latest political news with them.

There is a plot of sorts in *Letters on Various Interesting and Important Subjects.* The first letter, signed "Monarchist," claims that the governors of the people, by history and by natural right, can do as they please. Slender reveals in the second letter that he is puzzled by "Monarchist" and that he has decided to stop taking Fenno's Federalist paper, "not that I disliked his politics, but because he taught the children to *curse,* and speak *bawdy.*"[13] So he writes his intention to take Benjamin Bache's firmly Republican *Aurora* instead. As the letters continue, Slender, educated by his friend and neighbor the Latinist, becomes more firmly convinced that the *Aurora's* politics are the right ones, and supports them, albeit fearfully, in face of the scorn of the village, and his own fears of ostracism and of pursuit by minions of the Federalist government. The series ends with a strong and firm call by Slender to all honest men of the United States to support the Republicans, to oppose the Federalists, and to cast their votes proudly in the upcoming election. Thus Slender begins as an unthinking Federalist, becomes an unsure Republican, and finally ends as a firm and courageous one. As long as there are two opposing political parties, the humor of these letters will have validity.

In the introductory address, the Latinist serves as a foil for Slender, who has come to him to announce his project for publishing the letters. The Latinist, who tries to discourage him, objects because Slender is not rich, has no titles to string after his name, and no great patron. Slender solves these objections by declaring he will list himself as O. S. M. (One of the Swinish Multitude); then, in worrying about his dedication, he becomes vocal: "I'll dedicate to all their masters—To the Freemen of the United States; and I'll bet you a pair of boots, that my plain stories, shall be by them as well received, with my plain name, and O. S. M. as some of the productions of these flashy fellows, with a string of titles, which are of no other use to American freemen, than to lull them to sleep." For political purposes, Freneau evidently did not hesitate to appeal to any current anti-intellectualism. But Slender claims his purpose is to arouse the country "to a more ardent love of their country's rights—to more watchfulness, and to stricter enquiry," and such may also have been Freneau's justification.

The Slender of the dedication is, however, the "educated" Slender; in the beginning letters, he is still timorous about these heretical Republican notions; therefore, the ringing Republican declamation belongs to the Latinist. In Letter Two, Slender asks this neighbor to explain the "Monarchist." The Latinist admits that it is true about princes' having absolute power; then, becoming more and more oratorical, he declares that even if the rich in the United States are wicked, the American farmers still are virtuous: "but said my friend (leaping to his feet, whilst I shrunk into a corner) the sun will arise with ten-fold glory; the demons of war, discord, and desolation shall be disappointed—true religion shall banish pretence and hypocrisy, and AMERICA SHALL STILL BE FREE."

Slender's timorousness is constantly underlined. Since the evils that the Federalist papers predict for America are totally believed by him, he constantly fears a French invasion, a siege of burning and looting by the United Irishmen, and anarchy around the next corner. When he overhears two men in the tavern talk about an aristocrat and describe one as a great beast the English left behind after the war, Slender trembled on his way home, "looking on this side, and that, for fear it would leap upon me from some of its lurking places." Even in Letter Seven, well into the series, Slender is still fearful. He wants to flee somewhere for safety, for "our President, said I, said our country was in danger of being turned into a bedlam by French principles—But I doubt that we stand in more danger of turning it into a slaughterhouse by wicked practices." Slender's wife, however, does not want to leave; and the Latinist counsels moderation. A new fear hits Slender in the tenth letter, for he is horrified that his writings might be considered seditious. In the fifteenth letter, the Latinist warns against the reestablishment of monarchy in the United States; and Slender is once more overwhelmed: "God help us, said I, I feel very much afraid indeed; I think I see the red coats once more march along the Delaware—I think I hear the groans of freeborn Americans from the hulk of the Jersey prison ship—my blood runs cold."

In addition to fears created by his gullibility in believing all the news stories, Slender has other problems to contend with. He seems surrounded by local Federalists who disapprove of his writing for the *Aurora*. His cousin Simon Simple fears Slender will be contaminated by the *Aurora*'s Bache: "Why he is represented all

thro' this neighborhood as a most strange sort of a man, and
moreover suspected somehow of a kind of an inclination for
democracy, and writing and printing about liberty; and how that all
men ought to be equal, and that the present system, which (as Mr.
Fenno says) no body understands, is better than the good old kingly
government, which you know our wise fathers always loved."

Slender's fledgling faith in the Republican principles is also shak-
en by the diatribes of his neighbor, and the Latinist can hardly
calm him after Slender hears this statement which has been initiated
by a discussion of jury trial for traitors:

this country would have been yet happy under the king of Great Britain; but
we were such plagued fools as to give the designing fellows liberty to prate;
they stirred up the common people, and chiefly the hot-headed rebellious
Irish, by which means the detestable sin of resisting the Lord's anointed
was committed, and under this sin our whole country lies, and for this, and
this only, have we been punished with first, the *Hessian Fly*, second the
Yellow Fever, and lastly by *rebellion;* and yet, with all this before our eyes,
some of you wish to have these men freed, and talk about *juries* forsooth!
but we'll *jury* them, and judge them too.

Only when writing as Robert Slender does Freneau allow himself to
write such colloquial speeches, but such writing evinces his fine ear
for political demagoguery.

In discussing the case of Jonathan Robbins, an impressed sailor
(who may or may not have been an American) who had led a mutiny
on a British ship, Freneau allows the Latinist to speak sarcastically:
"but you must remember, this was a frigate belonging to his
Britannic Majesty; the chief supporter of order, good government,
humanity and religion in the world." But Slender is not allowed
such subtlety in his speeches—his reactions are consistent. When
the Latinist mentions how bad a precedent the case is, Slender says,
"I think, I see slavery rattling her chains and sharpening all her
instruments of torture—What shall we do?—how shall we escape? . . . Is there no help?" The Latinist advises against fleeing
and recommends the ballot box as the best help. Although Freneau
does not portray Slender as having an education beyond his character and station, he does permit him to confound the local minister in
debate, but only with the result that a neighbor tells Mrs. Slender,
"Mr. Slender is an infidel—a speaker against the clergy—a puller
down of religion—and his reverence says so!"

Letter Twenty-two, one of the best of Freneau's prose pieces, shows Slender as talking to himself on the way to the tavern:

Having heard that there was a tavern at about the distance of a mile or so from my favourite country spot, where now and then a few neighbours meet to spit, smoke segars, drink apple whiskey, cider, or cider-royal, and read the news—a few evenings ago, I put on my best coat, combed out my wig, put my spectacles in my pocket, and a quarter dollar—This I thought was right; for although Mrs. Slender told me eleven-pence was enough, says I, I'll e'en take the quarter dollar, for a man always feels himself of more consequence when he has got good money in his pocket—so out I walks, with a good stout stick in my hand, which I always make a point to carry with me, lest the dogs should make rather freer with my legs than I could wish. But I had not gone more than half the way, when, by making a false step, I splash'd my stocking from the knee to the ancle—Odds my heart, said I, see what a hand I have made of my stocking; I'll be bail, added I, I'll hear of this in both sides of my head—but it can't now be helped—this, and a thousand worse accidents, which daily happen, are all occasioned by public neglect, and the misapplication of the public's money—Had I, said I, (talking to myself all the while) the disposal of but half the income of the United States, I could at least so order matters, that a man might walk to his next neighbour's without splashing his stockings, or being in danger of breaking his legs in ruts, holes, gutts, and gullies. I do not know, says I to myself, as I moralized on my splash'd stocking, but money might with more profit be laid out in repairing the roads, than in marine establishments, supporting a standing army, useless embassies, exhorbitant salaries, given to many flashy fellows that are no honour to us, or to themselves, and chartering whole ships to carry a single man to another nation.

In this one paragraph, Freneau has characterized Slender as a man who is "one of us." While the trip to the tavern is humorous, we sympathize with Slender for his splashed stockings. The incident of the mudhole leads naturally to the diatribe about the government, and we again sympathize since this speech is a natural one that contains a natural reaction.

In the last letter, Freneau abandons his devices for involving Slender in dilemmas or dialogues; instead, he presents him as a political orator who is pleading with the public to cast their votes in the right way. The letter is a *tour de force*, for Slender tries to appeal to all, even while apparently shunning the votes of some:

Ye aristocrats, and great men, whether merchants, doctors, proctors, or lawyers, who sigh for greatness, and long for dominion, whose hearts yearn for the glory of a *Crown*, the splendor of a court, or the sweet marrow bones that are to be pick'd in his Majesty's kitchen—whose eyes ache painfully, once again to see the stars, crosses, crescents, coronets, with all the hieroglyphicals, enigmaticals, emblematicals, and all the other cals, including *rascals*, which adorn the court of kings—give a strong, true, and decided vote for James Ross, who supports, approves, hopes for, longs for, and sighs for all these.

Not exhausted by this one sentence, Slender later turns to those he favors, the multitude; and he directs their votes to McKean and Liberty.

The *Letters* are truly literary political propaganda. That Freneau, educated, refined, poetic, could enjoy creating Robert Slender is but another indication of his great versatility. Even though he promised that, if this volume sold successfully, a second volume would be published, it never appeared. The volume, as it stands, is a chronicle of Slender's political reactions to the governor's election of 1800—it comes to its natural conclusion with Letter Twenty-four. The education of Robert Slender had been completed.

Although Slender signatures continue to appear in the *Aurora* after the McKean-Ross election (most notably when Slender comments on the tie vote between Thomas Jefferson and Aaron Burr: "why, then the devil and A. H—lt—n are at the bottom of this balloting"), Freneau seems to have abandoned him in his later essay series. In 1804, when Tench Coxe led the Quids, a third party, against the Jeffersonian Republicans and the Federalists in Pennsylvania, Freneau adopted the Bunkers as spokesmen. The Bunkers were farmers who were less philosophical and who were more terrified of democracy, democrats, and Jeffersonians than Slender. But these letters do not have the charm of the Slender letters, possibly because they are negative, being anti-Coxe rather than pro-Republican. This time, finally, Freneau was an advocate of the "ins" after being so long on the offensive. Following the Bunker series, Freneau did little more with published prose. In 1816, he contributed a short observation about spots on the sun to the New York *Weekly Museum*, and in 1822 he adopted the tone of the old man, wise in the ways of the world, for "Recollections of Past Times and Events." While these contributions show his learning, his reading, and his skill as a stylist, they do not approach his greatest prose achievement—the character of Robert Slender, O. S. M.

CHAPTER 4

Poetry for Poetry's Sake

I The Retired Gentleman

WITH Jefferson's election to the presidency in 1800, Freneau withdrew to a great extent from public life and political controversy. He no longer traveled to New York or Philadelphia to aid the party's press, and he established no more newspapers to express his point of view. For the next few years he turned to his other vocation, the sea, in an effort to support his still growing family (his fourth daughter was born in 1801). Then he retired from the sea and devoted himself to the rural, contemplative life that he had celebrated in so many of his poems. In a letter to Madison, he describes his surroundings: "my walks have been confined, with now and then a short excursion, to the neighbourhood of the Never Sink hills, and under some old hereditary trees, and on some fields, which I well recollect for sixty years."[1]

Freneau seems to have been content with this life: he resumed his classical studies; continued reading and learning about the new developments in the science of the day; and, for intellectual companionship, journeyed to New York to become a part of the circle formed by Dr. John W. Francis, Dr. Samuel L. Mitchell, DeWitt Clinton, John Pintard—the chief members of the New York Historical and Philosophical Societies. Gradually Freneau sold more and more of the land of his estate; his brother, who had so often helped him financially, died; in 1818 his home burned; but little of this seems to have soured Freneau. Although he lost one lawsuit after another for debts owed to neighbors, his poetry reflected none of his financial distress. These years were calm ones; finally, he was able to devote himself to his poetry without being harassed by a newspaper deadline or by the necessity to publish a poem while the event it recorded was still fresh in the minds of the public. He had time now to revise his earlier poetry, to issue two new editions, and to pick and choose among his poems for those for which he wished to be remembered. These years were mellow ones for Freneau.

In Freneau's letter to his brother's partner of June 26, 1801, he mentions that some of his neighbors "have lately been in the whim of sending me to the legislature," but he adds that the public "have blockheads enough for that purpose."[2] Freneau's friends did not give up; for, in 1803, Francis Bailey of Philadelphia, discovering that a position in the New York post office was vacant, wrote to Madison suggesting that none "would fill the office with more ability, or greater integrity, than Philip Freneau."[3] Fortunately, by the time of this last letter, Freneau had a surer source of income since he had returned to the sea in 1802, this time in a joint venture with his brother: Philip captained the *John;* Peter owned it. Intended as a coastal cargo carrier, the *John* made but two round trips before the brothers sold the schooner and bought the brig *Washington,* which they planned to use for the Madeira wine trade that their father had engaged in years before. In these years, Freneau noted in his poetry little of contemporary events; he even seems to have ignored the election of 1808 in which his old friend Madison successfully ran for president. Times, and Freneau, had changed.

Most indicative of the changing times was the *Port Folio's* review of his 1795 volume of poetry in the fall of 1807. The *Port Folio,* generally considered staid, conservative, and Federalist, treated Freneau kindly—and such an attitude would have been unimaginable earlier. But he had now been silent for a number of years; and, although past quarrels were remembered, their violence was forgotten. The *Port Folio* concluded, rather verbosely: "of the *poetry* of this versatile bard we must say that, by the impartial, it will be at length, considered as entitled to no ordinary place in a judicious estimate of American genius."[4] Thus Freneau's name once again came before the public, as it did again in 1808, when the New Yorkers commemorated the burial of the bones of those who had died on the prison ships; for parts of "The British Prison Ship" were reprinted as well as his poem that mourned the dispersal of the prisoners' bones.

We are not surprised therefore, to find Freneau writing Madison in the spring of 1809 to inform him of plans to print a new edition of his poems: "I found last Winter an Edition would soon be going on at all events, and in contradiction to my wishes, as I had left these old scribblings, to float quietly down the stream of oblivion to their destined element the ocean of forgetfulness. . . . I am endeavouring to make the whole work as worthy of the public eye as circumstances will allow. 1500 copies are to be printed, only; but I have a certainty, from the present popular frenzy, that three times that number might soon be disposed of."[5]

Whether the public was indeed "frenzied" we do not know, but we do know that Freneau never complained that this edition, *Poems written and published during the American Revolutionary War*, did not sell. Both Freneau and his publishers must have decided that the time was right for his poetry, for "Slender's Journey" was also republished. His prose, though, was a different matter. Evidently Madison had suggested that he include some such pieces in the new volume, but Freneau did not like the idea; he suspected that "anything I have written in that way is so inferior to the Poetry, that the contrast will be injurious to the credit of the Publication."[6] Freneau was evidently determined that this volume, at least, would confirm his worth as a poet.

It is very possible that Freneau intended this 1809 volume as the capstone of his career, for he was poetically silent until 1814, when he began publishing some occasional poems in New Jersey newspapers. Freneau, so vocal during the Revolutionary War against Great Britain, was unusually silent during the War of 1812 about the same enemy. From the evidence of his *A Collection of Poems, On American Affairs* of 1815, we can conclude that he was writing poetry to commemorate the events of the war but that he did not choose to publish it until after the war. Possibly, like his New York literary friends, men of the "old" school, he had regarded the war as unnecessary and had given little support to it.

But at the end of the war he did publish his last volume, *A Collection of Poems, on American Affairs*, containing, as he told Madison, "poems on different subjects, moral, political, or merely amusing, and not a few upon the events of the times since May 1812."[7] Despite the care and time Freneau devoted to the publication, he was not rewarded by any great sales. As he commented to Dr. Francis the next year, he was "not a little out of humour that my two little volumes seemed to have fallen nearly deadborn from the press, owing to the enmity of some, the politics of others, and the general inattention of all."[8] He expresses his bitterness over the criticism his poems had received; apparently his politics were still held against him, for some readers found fault with poems about

Paine and about Jefferson. But Freneau ascribes much of the book's lack of success to the cultural level of the city itself: "what use for poetry where men have no idea of its efficacy and influence over the human mind."[9]

Lack of financial success never kept Freneau from writing poetry. In the same letter to Dr. Francis, he mentions a contemplated poem about the Elgin Gardens, which he had visited while in New York; and he announces yet another volume of poetry: "I am transcribing a poem of about 1400 lines on the Repulse of the British Army from New Orleans in January last. . . . Mr. Longworth, or rather Nicholas Van Riper, will set about printing it in about three weeks."[10] It was to be a small volume, for it was to contain only the New Orleans poem and a few others that were to be added, and Freneau was to return to New York on June 10, apparently to supervise the printing; but, unfortunately, the volume has never been found: it may never have been printed.

Freneau did, however, print several poems in the *New York Mirror* in the fall of 1816; and he probably continued his occasional visits to New York, where Dr. Francis seems to have been his patron. Certainly the friendship continued through 1822, when Francis apparently asked to see Freneau's proposals for a new volume of his verse, and he may even have offered to act as a go-between for the poet with the printer. This time, however, the effort was in vain, for we hear nothing of this volume which was intended to emphasize Freneau's Revolutionary War verse.

The year 1822 was one of literary resurgence for Freneau, for he also turned again to prose. "Recollections of Past Times and Events" appeared in four installments in the Trenton *True American* in the fall. These essays, describing minor aspects of the war and of his journeys, indicate that, if the generation that had experienced the Revolutionary War was dying, a new one was interested in it. In these later years, Freneau published intermittently; and during the years 1821–1824 a number of his verses appeared in New York and New Jersey papers—possibly published this way because the publication of the hoped-for 1822 volume did not materialize. The last date on a Freneau poem is 1827, and his last signature appears on his application for a pension for his Revolutionary War service in August, 1832. Freneau's death on December 18, 1832, concluded a long and remarkably productive life. In the years since 1800 he had kept alive his reputation as a poet, especially that of "the poet of the

Revolution"; and he had lived down, to some extent, his reputation as a radical. He had gone over his poems, choosing, editing, revising them for the public of his time, and for posterity. He made it clear, in these later years, that he wished to be remembered as a poet, not as an essayist or a party newspaper editor.

II *Time for Poetry*

In the twenty years between 1795 and 1815, Freneau supervised the printing of three editions of his poetry—one, in 1795, he printed himself. While not carbon copies, the 1795 *Poems: Written between the Years 1768 & 1794* and *Poems written and published during the American Revolutionary War* (1809) have a similar content; and the 1815 volume, *A Collection of Poems on American Affairs*, contains poems previously uncollected, those written since 1797. Of special interest is the 1795 single volume, for this volume Freneau printed at Mount Pleasant. For it, Freneau went over his poetry and made major revisions: his famous "House of Night" became "Vision of Night," while "The Power of Fancy" became two poems, "Fancy's Ramble" and "Ode to Fancy." The volume also shows Freneau's care to preserve those poems he had written many years before; and we suspect that he sought to make use of every line that had some value in it. The volume, a chronicle of his interests, is a representative collection containing poetry of all his various styles and moods.

In this collection, Freneau orders his poems in a roughly chronological manner. His poems written in college, such as "Rising Glory of America" and "The Pyramids of Egypt," appear first. "The Vision of Night," "The Wild Honey-Suckle," and "The Vanity of Human Existence" are grouped together, as are his early poems against the British. "The Beauties of Santa Cruz" appears before a grouping of the later Revolutionary War poems—"Eutaw Springs" and "The British Prison Ship" are, of course, included. The war poems are relieved by a group of poems now known as the "Amanda" poems, dedicated to, or concerning, a young lady of that name, although originally they often bore other feminine names. The poems of his seaboard trading, along with those written about South Carolina, are interrupted by "Slender's Journey" and the newly formed "Fancy's Ramble." He also includes the poems of the period of his newspaper editing: the occasional poems dealing with the French Revolution, as well as the satires against his Federalist opponents. Although we can discern these groups and this vague ordering by date of composition, Freneau evidently sought to achieve variety in each section, for he never let one type of poem predominate for many pages.

"Variety" is even more the key descriptive word for the edition of 1809. Although the poems are the same (with few exceptions) as in the 1795 edition, they were extensively reordered; about the only constant grouping is the "Amanda" poems. Although the table of contents was so thoroughly revised, the poems were not. Freneau corrected obvious mistakes, rewrote a line here and there, and this reissue of the 1795 volume contained fewer poems of controversy. The full title of this 1809 edition emphasizes what Freneau thought would appeal: *Poems: written and published during the American Revolutionary War, and now republished from the original Manuscripts; interspersed with Translations from the Ancients, and other Pieces not heretofore in Print.* Both in this title and in the advertisement of the volumes great emphasis is placed on the Revolutionary War poems, although they constitute less than half of the volume. In the advertisement, Freneau mentions that a few later poems have been inserted, "but not so as to materially interrupt the general tenor of the Poems that arose from the incidents of the American revolutionary contest."[11]

Although the emphasis on the war poems is not new, the emphasis on "Translations from the Ancients" is. Perhaps 1809 was the right moment for both genres to be successful with the public. Both classifications, however, look backward to past triumphs and tastes, not forward. Freneau was working on this summary of his work during the same summer that Washington Irving was composing his *Knickerbocker's History of New York,* a work which satirized contemporary conditions and which indicated the rise of a new author and a new style.

A Collection of Poems, on American Affairs, and a variety of other Subjects, chiefly moral and political; written between the Year 1797 and the present Time, which Freneau published in 1815, did not, for a change, rely on the inclusion of his Revolutionary War poems to attract the reader, although "By Philip Freneau, Author of Poems written during the Revolutionary War" was carried on the title page. Although this edition contains the variety common to Freneau's other volumes, the total impression is different, possibly because the proportion of satiric poems is greatly lessened. There are a greater number of didactic poems in this volume than the others. Freneau writes on Good Fortune, Superstition, and Happiness; there are a number of poems discussing the nature of the universe. In this volume, there is more abstract discussion of nature and less delineation of individual scenes and events in the natural world. Throughout the volume, Freneau experiments with various lengths of line and with various rhyme schemes and meters; and he achieves an entire volume of skillful verse in which we find few awkwardnesses.

These three volumes of Freneau's poetry, all published with his supervision, provide the basis for a discussion of those poems which Freneau sought to keep alive. Much of the verse, collected this way, was the occasional poetry already discussed. Although these poems were also revised for the later editions, their form at the time of composition and first publication in the journals of the day is most important. But, for the large body of nonoccasional poems, we must look to these later editions; for he was undoubtedly a better poet in his later years than in the college or war years. Some of Freneau's best-known poems were improved by the revisions made in these late years when he had time for poetry.

III *"The House of Night," "The Power of Fancy"*

Somewhat unfortunately for Freneau's reputation, two of his best-known nonoccasional poems, "The House of Night" and "The Power of Fancy," are among his earliest work and are studied in their earlier forms; it is unfortunate because these two poems in particular improved with Freneau's revisings. Both of these poems have been shown to be extremely imitative of English verse. Harry Hayden Clark in "Literary Influences" has indicated Freneau's debt in "The House of Night" to Thomas Gray, Edward Young, Hugh Blair, and Thomas Sackville. Gray's is the stanza form, but the message is adapted from Young's "Night Thoughts on Death and Immortality" and from Blair's "The Grave." Freneau's poem exists, however, in three states; and each is different enough from the others to entitle it to be considered as a separate poem.

When "The House of Night" was first published in 1779, it consisted of seventy-three stanzas. In it, the speaker recounts a poetic vision: he is led one gloomy night to a house with lights ablaze, he enters, and he passes a group of doctors in the anteroom who are quarreling over the correct medication to give their patient. The patient, the speaker discovers to his horror, is Death. Death speaks to him of the wars, the famines, and the gloom which are his companions; and he asks for the Holy Book and sacred authors to read for consolation. But the speaker denies any peace for Death, for it is written that Hell and Death must perish. Death then asks the poet-speaker to engrave his epitaph, which he dictates, upon his tombstone. While the speaker is on his way to do so, he hears Death give a last howl and sees him buried. The speaker is stooping to write the epitaph when the scene disappears.

The poem concludes with a reference to the power of Fancy and with a meditation on immortality. The reader is asked if he fears death and is then assured by the poet that the New Jordan "will but waft thee where thy fathers are." The speaker then cites his own lack of fear: "when God and nature give the word,/ I'll tempt the dusky shore and narrow sea:/ Content to die, just as it be decreed,/ At four score years, or now at twenty-three." This 1779 poem is, therefore, a fairly unified one of religious melancholy. Freneau does utilize some of the graveyard trappings when his speaker approaches the house and when he departs from it, but most of the horror stems from the thought of the evil of death, and the poem concludes with the peace of the triumph over death in afterlife.

The best-known version of "The House of Night," that of 1786, has a much different emphasis. Freneau fills this version with more action and more dialogue: they almost double the poem's length. The introductory stanzas attribute the vision of Death to Fancy, whose power exerts itself when the poet sleeps: "Thou play'st thy wild delusive part so well/ You lift me into immortality,/ Depict new heavens, or draw the scenes of hell." Appropriately for a poem on the death of Death, Fancy's power is a night power, exerted completely only when "Reason holds no sway." Having given the speaker the right to depart from reason's bounds, Freneau, as in the earlier version, sends him to the house which is surrounded by "a mournful garden of autumnal hue" and which includes those graveyard stalwarts, "the yew, the myrtle, and the church-yard elm,/ The cypress, with its melancholy green." The poet in the poem proceeds as before, past the doctors, into the room of Death, whom he describes:

> Sad was his countenance, if we can call
> That countenance, where only bones were seen
> And eyes sunk in their sockets, dark and low,
> And teeth, that only show'd themselves to grin.

At this point, Freneau introduces a new character who is not in the

1779 version, Cleon, owner of the house Death is inhabiting. Cleon explains that he is giving what comfort he can to the dying Death, and he asks the poet to do likewise since " 'the bleeding Saviour of a world undone/ Bade thy compassion rise toward thy foe.' " To stress Cleon's charity in thus aiding Death, Freneau has Cleon tell the poet of the ills that Death has brought him. Cleon's complaint, in the form of a typical pre-Romantic love elegy, relates that Death has stolen Aspasia, "she the loveliest of her kind," from Cleon. Her death is described in unoriginal terms:

> "Sweet as the fragrance of the vernal morn,
> Nipt in its bloom this faded flower I see;
> The inspiring angel from that breast is gone,
> And life's warm tide forever chill'd in thee!"

Thus to the melancholy surroundings of the house and the sight of Death is added the new melancholy of love lost.

The poet now takes over the Death-watch and does what he can to ease Death's pain. He fetches him medicine, water, and helps him walk; but Death's pain is not eased. Death then awakens Cleon and requests, as in the 1779 version, the holy writings. Cleon, who gives the response, reminds Death of all his past misdeeds, the present death of Aspasia, and the future deaths to be accomplished by the coming Hessians and British. There can be no peace for Death. Death, despairing, agrees and asks for an undertaker in order to give him directions for his coffin. The exchange between the undertaker and Death is seriocomic, for the undertaker wants to make sure of his pay before beginning his work. The poem, all too soon, returns, however, to the dominating melancholy tone, as Death dictates his epitaph, with a proper moral application:

> *"Traveller, wouldst thou his noblest trophies seek,*
> *Search in no narrow spot obscure for those;*
> *The sea profound, the surface of all land*
> *Is moulded with the myriads of his foes."*

Upon this conclusion, a wind rises, nature becomes distorted:

> Lights in the air like burning stars were hurl'd,
> Dogs howl'd, heaven mutter'd, and the tempest blew,
> The red half-moon peeped from behind a cloud
> As if in dread the amazing scene to view.

No writer of the Gothic would be ashamed of these lines.

Despite Nature's fury, however, the poet proceeds to the graveyard of a nearby church to engrave the epitaph; and, while on his way, he is able still to see Death in his agonies ("For fancy gave to my enraptur'd soul/ An eagle's eye"). Undeterred by this sight, the poet continues to the church, where he sees the funeral procession and the burial. As in the earlier version, when the poet begins to write the epitaph, the vision ends; and the poet concludes with the moral. This application, though, is different. Nelson Adkins[12] has pointed out the Lucretian nature of the definition of death as "one unceasing change":

> Hills sink to plains, and man returns to dust,
> That dust supports a reptile or a flower;
> Each changeful atom by some other nurs'd
> Takes some new form, to perish in an hour.

But, in the very last stanza, Freneau returns to the more doctrinal message of the first ending: "When Nature bids thee from the world retire,/ With joy thy lodging leave, a fated guest;/ In Paradise, the land of thy desire,/ Existing always, always to be blest."

This 1786 "House of Night" is a much more dramatic poem than the earlier version, for the poet in the poem becomes an actor rather than an observer. Death also becomes more active; and Cleon, while helping Death, is nevertheless his vocal enemy. The major action and the realism of it, while adding interest to the poem, detract from the allegorical intention of the poem. Death is a shade too human. The minor action is also realistic—the fetching of the medicine, the insistence of the undertaker on his pay, and Death's complaints. But these acts make us think of Death as a patient dying instead of inducing awe at the death of Death. Cleon's story of Aspasia with its gentle melancholy also detracts from the allegory. Even the moral gives two ways of accepting Death—scientifically and theologically. What the 1786 version gains in drama and realism it loses in unity.

Evidently Freneau was dissatisfied with his 1786 poem, either because of its message or its length; for in 1795 he retained only a few of its stanzas when he created "The Vision of the Night—A Fragment." This title is indeed descriptive of the poem, for it becomes essentially a fanciful night wandering. Fancy, who again dominates the poet's sleeping hours, leads him to mournful surroundings where he sees the lighted house. Now, instead of entering, the poet continues to the church which is described as before

as built by sinners and which is thereby endowed with its own
horror. There the poem ends. Freneau thus retains the Gothic
machinery, the description of plants and places calculated to rouse
horror and melancholy, but he omits the message. There is no
address to the reader either for him to take heed or for him to look
beyond death; in fact, Death is not even mentioned. The 1795 poem
stands merely as an example of the poetic fancy.

Freneau celebrated the ability of Fancy in another early poem,
"The Power of Fancy," which Professor Clark designates as an
example of Freneau's imitativeness—this time of Joseph Warton's
"Ode to Fancy."[13] "The Power of Fancy," according to Freneau,
was written in 1770; and this version of the poem is the one usually
studied. However, in his definitive 1809 edition, he divided the
poem in two, producing "Fancy's Ramble," which once more follows Warton's plan, and "Ode to Fancy," which is probably one of
Freneau's better poems. "Ode to Fancy" consists of the first twenty
and the last fourteen lines of the original "The Power of Fancy."
These stanzas, detached in this way from the first poem, create an
amazingly unified and satisfactory poem. The first stanza deals with
Fancy's origin and nature:

> Wakeful, vagrant, restless thing,
> Ever wandering on the wing,
> Who thy wondrous source can find,
> Fancy, regent of the mind;
> A spark from Jove's resplendent throne,
> But thy nature all unknown.

The second group of lines produces the implied comparison between the products of man's fancy and those of "the Power Divine":
"What is this globe, these lands, and seas,/ . . . / But thoughts on
reason's scale combin'd,/ Ideas of the Almighty mind!" The last
stanza deals with Fancy as "the muses' pride" and recounts her
contributions to the poets' powers:

> By thee Elysian groves were made,
> Thine were the notes that Orpheus play'd;
> By thee was Pluto charm'd so well
> While rapture seiz'd the crowds of hell—

Then the last two lines ask Fancy to accompany the poet himself:
"Come, O come—perceiv'd by none,/ You and I will walk alone."

Despite these last two lines, the poem is more Miltonic than Romantic; for there is little sensuousness present, and the poem is too much a product of reason—to intellectual. However, "Ode to Fancy" with its simplicity and comparisons is a very good poem.

The remaining lines of "The Power of Fancy," much revised, make up "Fancy's Ramble" in Freneau's later editions. To replace the first lines which he had used for "Ode to Fancy," Freneau composed a new introduction in which he once more describes the nature of Fancy. As in "Ode to Fancy," the poet's feelings are not involved in the poem—the poet merely accompanies Fancy as she exhibits her powers. As in "The Power of Fancy," the ramble is a territorial one. Fancy brings "images of absent things," and she journeys to Arcadia, "*Hecla's* high and smoky steep," Norway, Ossian's Caledonia, Granada, the Amazon, the Canaries, Britain, the Ganges, China, the islands of the Pacific. The journey concludes, as in "The Power of Fancy," with a visit to a tomb where Fancy's powers to "pierce the shade" are illustrated. Freneau ends "Fancy's Ramble" by questioning the permanence of Marcella's death; and he concludes that her eyes, "Like heaven's bright lamp, beneath the main/ They are but set, to rise again."

"Fancy's Ramble" is an improvement over the lines taken from "The Power of Fancy." The journey is shorter, and the lines contain less of the Gothic machinery and sentiment. Fancy no longer "walks upon the moon" or listens to the music "of the bright, harmonious spheres." She no longer visits "some lonely dome,/ Where Religion loves to come," nor does she descend to "the prison of the fiends." Ossian is fortunately no longer referred to as "sweetest Ossian," and Freneau for some reason omits one of the more famed lines, "Sappho, Lesbos mourns for thee." The visit to the tomb is much improved, for there was something grisly in the original about the poet's requesting Fancy to "let me glide as well as you/ Through the shroud and coffin too." "Fancy's Ramble" is less melancholy than "The Power of Fancy," for the poem concentrates more upon positive values than upon mourning past poets and heroes. Freneau's revisions of "The Power of Fancy" demonstrate his improvement in poetic perception.

IV *Poetry in the Melancholy Tradition—Poems on Love*

Despite Freneau's complaint in "To Sylvius" that in America "no taste for plaintive elegy is known,/ Nor lyric ode—none care for

things like these," he himself wrote many of these two types of
poetry during all periods of his life. The elegies on unfortunate love
and on death, the graveyard musings, the poems on the vanity of
existence, and the poems celebrating retirement from the world
form a major part of Freneau's nonoccasional verse. Whether these
poems were written because they suited the taste of the day for
melancholy poetry or whether Freneau's own taste dictated these
subjects is hard to discover. We do know that, for every type of
poem written in the melancholy manner, there is at least one
mocking that genre and the taste that supported it. And we know
from his occasional verse that he wrote poems on almost any event
that crossed his path. It seems natural, therefore, that Freneau
would write much in the fashionable pre-Romantic style, a style
which encouraged sensitivity of emotion; but he never became a
Romantic—he never bared his soul; he kept himself detached from
his poems. Morover, his poems mocking the pre-Romantic genre
demonstrate his convictions that reason and proportion should rule.
His melancholy poetry is generally derivative. Although in later
editions he revised and improved it, the poems of real interest
remain those which mock the tradition.

For his 1809 edition, Freneau revised a group of his early poems,
the love elegies. These poems, as originally published, were addressed to, or were about, girls with a variety of classical names. For
the 1809 edition, Freneau grouped them together as the "Amanda"
poems. Although he changed the titles and the names, the poems
still illustrate his early imitativeness of the fashionable melancholy
poetry. Bearing all too close a resemblance to Della Cruscan poetry
to be popular today, such poems attempt to evoke the melancholy of
lost love or of lovers parted, usually by the vagaries of the sea. "The
Bermuda Islands" pictures Amanda searching the sea for her lover's
ship: "Now, on some rock, with loose, dishevelled hair,/ Near
dashing waves, the sorrowing beauty stands." "Florio to Amanda"
serves as a companion piece, for in it we have the melancholy fears
of Florio that he should not have left Amanda to go to sea. His only
consolation is "by Fancy's aid, to unseen coasts repair,/ And fondly
dwell on absent beauty there."

"Philander: Or the Emigrant" is connected to the "Amanda"
poems because Philander strayed from Amanda and her warm
climate and found that Lavinia, in a more northern region, was as
fair. The two new lovers, however, must soon part; for Philander
must return to sea:

> To the bleak shore the parting lovers came,
> And while Philander did his sighs renew,
> So near the deep they bade their last farewell
> That the rough surge, to quench the mutual flame
> Burst in and broke the embrace, and o'er Lavinia flew;
> While a dark cloud hung lowering o'er the main,
> From whence the attendants many an omen drew,
> And said Philander would not come again!

And, though "oft' to the winding shore Lavinia came," Philander did not come again, leaving Lavinia to mourn. In view of the original desertion of Philander, perhaps the lament in the poem "Amanda's Complaint" is justified. Having aided the visiting mariner, she demands that he admit that the girls of the southern region are as fair as those of the northern in a poem that is obviously of a lighter nature than the others of the group. More melancholy is "The Fair Solitary," titled in 1795 "The Mourning Nun." In it we find not only the inherent melancholy of the lost-love theme but learn that Florio was a deceiver, who left the girl her "frail virtue to deplore." Nothing can give her back her cheerfulness: "Vain are those drugs that art and love prepares,/ No art redeems the waste of sighs and tears!"

In English verse, the effects of lost love are often tragic for the heroine, and so they are in Freneau's verse. For the 1809 edition, Freneau adapted the poem "To Marcia," which had originally appeared as a mock example of such melancholy tastes, and changed it to "Amanda in Consumption." Amanda, as Marcia was, is inconsolably melancholy but with reason; she seems to be suffering "with fevers brought from sultry climes." Amanda dies ("So, to the grave Amanda goes,/ Her whole duration—but an hour!"); and the poet realizes he has not lived in vain, "for, slighting all the sages knew,/ I learn philosophy from you." The poem is defective and is one example of a revision that did not improve the original poem. More unified in tone is "Elegaic Lines," which commemorates Amanda's death; and it is more unified despite the fact that here Freneau combined two previously separate poems. The poem begins and ends with a moral. We are first told to imitate Amanda's example and be resigned to death; the final moral is directed to "ye thoughtless fair" who should take warning from this example of perished beauty. In between the two morals, Freneau praises Amanda's virtue and beauty, with traditional exaggeration. Amanda is used primarily as an example that all things, no matter how

beautiful, must die: "Yet, not her virtues, opening into bloom,/ Nor
all her sweetness saved her from the tomb." This poem completes
Amanda's story.

Although some have read the "Amanda" poems as the biography
of Freneau's love for a Bermudian, the fact that so few of Freneau's
feelings enter the poems gives us little assurance about this sup-
position. If Freneau experienced the emotion and loss he describes,
he conceals it well behind the conventions of Romantic melancholy.
There is, however, one love elegy which does reveal more emotion
or which at least conveys more real emotion to the reader. Significantly, this poem is not included in the "Amanda" poems, although it might well have been, since it deals with the theme of the
sea as a barrier between parted lovers. The poem first appeared
without title in 1789, but it was named "To Cynthia" in the edition
of 1809. Admittedly, the poem begins as artificially as the others, for
the sailor, having left Cynthia, envies the stream where she lives:
"how blest art thou/ To kiss the bank where she resides." The
remainder of the poem, while still employing conventional
melancholy attitudes, uses specifics not usually found in such
poems. The poet prizes a memento of Cynthia, "the painted toy/
That near my careless heart you hung." But, "fettered fast in icy
fields," neither the ship nor the sailor can progress on the journey
home:

> Yet, still in hopes of vernal showers,
> And breezes, moist with morning dew,
> I pass the lingering, lazy hours,
> Reflecting on the spring—and you.

In this last stanza Freneau does catch something of the boredom of
the sailors with little to do while on a ship in port. Despite the
melancholy machinery of the beginning, the conclusion is neither
dreary nor melancholy, for a reasonable man is patient.

Knowledge of the rest of Freneau's work should lead us to suspect
that, even though he wrote poems in this melancholy genre and
thought enough of them to retain them in the 1809 version, he
would scorn any real-life Amandas or Florios. Indeed, several of his
poems, both early and late, mock the conventions of the melancholy
love poem. In "A Modern Miracle," a poem from his 1788 volume
which has been undeservedly little discussed, Florella is the
melancholy heroine. The poem opens with Florella's speaking of her

malaise, her discomfort, her fears of passing from this world. Sir
Gilbert, a doctor who is attending her, suggests bleeding, which he
puts into effect. One more despairing, languid speech by Florella
follows before she loses consciousness. Sir Gilbert, struck by the
horror of the situation, has her moved from her chair to a nearby
couch; the servants, mourning, pay their last respects to their
mistress and leave the room. Sir Gilbert, however, in order to
express his much greater grief, remains. The concluding lines
present his actions:

> Like *Orpheus*, he, by passion led,
> Explor'd the kingdoms of the dead,
> Reliev'd the fainting maid so fair,—
> Out-doctor'd death—and got an heir!

The whole poem becomes an elaborate joke with a surprise ending
in which the melancholy is used to heighten the reversal.

Freneau again attacks the melancholy taste in the poem "Constantia." Like his "Fair Solitary," Constantia, weary of the world,
has determined to become a nun: " 'My happiness is all delayed—/
I'll go, and find it in the shade.' " A sailor tries to dissuade her:
" 'The druids' oak and hermits' pine/ Afford a gloomy, sad delight;/
But why that blush of health resign,/ The mingled tint of red and
white?' " The sailor's arguments are effective; Constantia agrees to
forego the nunnery and now pities any other "who seeks the shade."
In "Constantia," realism prevails over the melancholy fashion.

Two of Freneau's last poems also deal lightly with unhappy love.
In "The Fortunate Blacksmith," the smith is scorned by the lady;
and he, as all lovers should, threatens to drown himself—but to do
so in his tempering trough rather than in the more conventional sea.
The lady continues to refuse until the smith wins a lottery prize, and
then the two are married. In "Letitia," the companion piece to "The
Fortunate Blacksmith," the girl is scorned by the smith with dire
effects: "She griev'd and she groan'd, and had like to have died;/
Some thought she would quickly depart." But Letitia soon forsakes
the melancholy attitude, buys a lottery ticket, and wins a prize. The
blacksmith now courts her but gets this refusal: "When I lov'd you,
why did you love not?/ Your hand should have join'd to my hand on
that day,/ Should have struck when the iron was hot!" Of course, in
these last poems Freneau is poking fun at more subjects than the
convention of melancholy love; but his attitude in them, detached

and mocking, is more characteristic of Freneau than are the "Amanda" poems.

V *Lamentations and Graveyard Musings*

Since Freneau was essentially an occasional poet who felt compelled to express himself in verse on every event that interested him, we are not surprised to find a large number of verses commemorating deaths. This fact does not necessarily place him as a member of the school of melancholy, as his love elegies do; for, before poetic melancholy became fashionable, monodies on deaths were almost a requisite of the poet's art. Freneau's poem, "Stanzas to the Memory of General Washington," gives a good idea of the form usually followed in such commemorative verse. He first announces the death, then describes Washington as having departed for a more exalted sphere. The next duty of the poet seems to be to describe the man's accomplishments; in this instance, Washington is compared to heroes of the ancient world. Mention is made of the gratitude of those he served and of their sense of bereavement—none can replace him. The conclusion returns to the beginning theme—Washington has been exalted. Most of Freneau's commemorative verses on the great and famous fit this pattern.

But Freneau, always the man of reason, believed in keeping his comparisons and effusions restrained; that others did not is shown by Freneau's poem, "Stanzas Occasioned by certain absurd, extravagant, and even blasphemous panegyics and enconiums on the character of the late Gen. Washington," and the more humorous "Epistle from Dr. Franklin (deceased) to his Poetical Panegyrists, on some of their Absurd Compliments." The burden of the "Epistle" is that if, as the poets would have it, Nature wept for Franklin, she also wept for a beggar who died the same day; and, as Franklin points out, that day skies were clear in Carolina. In short, he has Franklin say, "reason should your pens direct/ Or else you pay me no respect." Freneau may have imbibed the spirit of Franklin's satiric "A Receipt to make a New-England Funeral Elegy" in the Dogood papers.

One of Freneau's poems about the death of the great and famous is quite unconventional. "Stanzas On the Decease of Thomas Paine," while exalting Paine and celebrating his accomplishments, denies the necessity for mourning not because of the usual anticipated heavenly bliss of the subject, but because Paine will continue to trouble earthly rascals. With a rollicking form and a repetitive refrain, the ballad commemorates Paine's abilities and predicts that they are not forever dead:

> To tyrants and the tyrant crew,
> Indeed, he was the bane;
> He writ, and gave them all their due,
> And signed it,—Thomas Paine.

> Oh! how we loved to see him write
> And curb the race of Cain!
> They hope and wish that Thomas P——
> May never rise again.

> What idle hopes!—yes—such a man
> May yet appear again.—
> When they are dead, they die for aye:
> —Not so with Thomas Paine.

The tone of the poem is almost one of defiance. Perhaps it is fitting that Freneau's verses about Paine's death were in the common ballad style, since Paine himself wrote for the masses.

But Freneau wrote commemorative verses not only for the great and famous but also for the lowly and unknown. "Stanzas to Robert Sevier and William Sevier," "On the Death of a Master Builder," "On the Loss of the Packet Ship Albion. Captain Williams, of New York," are only a few of the lesser-known titles. Most of these, like "Epitaph: On a Worthy Person," follow the conventions. For this poem, he follows the example of the epitaph in Gray's "Elegy," for Freneau's poem asks "some friendly eye, that views this ground," to "drop a tender tear." But the conclusion forbids being too melancholy, for "the mind to brighter regions soars,/ And acts and thinks for nobler ends."

In the late "Susanna's Tomb," the tone is not that of mild melancholy but of a stronger grief. The poem concerns the death of a ten-year-old girl whom the poet in the poem found dead on his return from "far Madeira's isle": "I thought to meet the expected smile—/ That smile I find forever fled,/ For all is serious with the dead." We look for the usual declaration that the dead one is now content in heavenly realms, but we find only a question: "Who now shall meet that smile of thine,/ The image once supposed divine." All the poet can do for the little one is tend the grave, "with heart of gloom/ To plant the trees that shade the tomb." The conclusion of the poem, instead of repeating the assurance of the heavenly state, pictures village maidens coming with flowers: "And every year their visit pay/ To deck the sod that hides your clay." The poem is a harsh one—no comfort is given. The poet limits Susanna to her tomb, to clay, to sod. Perhaps because of its harshness, the poem conveys real grief.

The poet of melancholy did not limit his mourning to humans; animals' deaths also served as appropriate subjects. In Freneau's "The Wanderer," he mourns a "songster of the feather'd kind" who is encountered in midocean. The bird is addressed by Thyrsis, who begs, " 'weak wanderer, trust the traitor, Man,/ And take the help that we bestow.' " The bird, however, "worn with wandering, droop'd her wing,/ And life resign'd in empty air." This early poem appeals deliberately to the current taste for melancholy—all is sentiment. But Freneau also mocked, as Gray did in "Ode on a Favourite Cat," this taste in "On a Honey Bee Drinking from a Glass of Wine and Drowned Therein." The poem is similar to Gray's, for an insignificant animal is elevated to the status of man and is assumed to be capable of receiving the poet's moralizings. First the poet welcomes the bee to his glass: "Here, be all care resigned.—/ This fluid never fails to please,/ And drown the griefs of men or bees." With this welcome, however, comes a warning: "Yet take not, oh! too deep a drink,/ And in this ocean die;/ Here bigger bees than you might sink,/ Even bees full six feet high." If the bee does not heed the warning, the poet promises him a tear as an epitaph and concludes, "go, take your seat in Charon's boat,/ We'll tell the hive, you died afloat." The poem is one of the best of Freneau's lighter poetry.

Another, but less well-known, poem skillfully interweaves the mocking of the melancholy epitaph for an animal with Freneau's rebellion against the habit of journalists of commemorating any unusual death. "On a Man Killed by a Buffaloe," which is included in the 1809 edition, comments on this journalistic tendency. After listing some of the means by which men meet their ends, the poet declares: "hard is their fate, but how much harder thine/ [who] were met, attacked, were conquered by a cow!" The poet complains that Fate should have awarded the man a set of horns, too, so the man could have won the contest, "and future times on the recording stone/ Had read, Here lies THE MAN THAT KILLED A COW."

However, Fate did not so decree, and there is only one recourse: "Now when the cow thinks fit her life to yield,/ If newsmen tell when she her race has ran,/ We'll raise her tomb in yonder flowery field,/ And write, HERE LIES THE COW THAT KILLED A MAN." Both Freneau's play of fancy and his sense of the ridiculous tempt him again and again to mock the conventions by extending them so far that they become comic.

Freneau produced very few graveyard poems *per se* despite the fact that he was actively writing in the years between 1790 and 1810 which mark the height of popularity of Gray's "Elegy." Having noted Freneau's melancholy verse and its imitativeness, his poems about graves and graveyards surprise, because they do not seek to produce that fashionable pensive melancholy. "On Passing by an Old Churchyard," from the 1815 edition, uses Gray's line but not Gray's stanza. The beginning does indeed resemble Gray's mood: "Pensive, on this green turf I cast my eye,/ And almost feel inclined to muse and sigh:/ Such tokens of mortality so nigh." But the mood quickly changes, for the poet in the poem asks whether those buried there are deserving of his melancholy: "Can we on such a kindred tear bestow?/ They, who, in life, were every just man's foe,/ A plague to all about them!" But the poet has second thoughts about his harshness because one honest man may be buried there; and for his sake "we would on knaves themselves bestow a tear,/ Think nature form'd them on some crooked plan,/ And say, peace rest on all that slumber here." This use of "one honest man" turns the poem into an Old Testament homily that reminds us of Abraham's pleading for Sodom and Gomorrah. Despite the promised tear for the sinners, the poem is not melancholy.

"Pewter-Platter Alley" is more conventional in language, although not in mood. The first stanza attempts to evoke the horror of a graveyard: "The people of that gloomy place/ In penance for some ancient crime/ Are held in a too narrow space." But there is greater fear that "he who treads this frozen ground/ Shall curse the chance that brought him here—/ The slippery mass predicts his fate,/ A broken arm, a wounded pate." In a return to the conventional, the watchman is described as avoiding the region, "for who would wish to wake the dead!" But Freneau adds a more reasonable explanation: the watchman does not come here for the dead "pay no tax to know the time." The place is deserted, but only because of the cold: "All, all to warmer regions flee,/ And leave the glooms to Towne and me." "Pewter-Platter Alley," although describing a graveyard, is essentially a poem of the city, depicting its life and habits by describing the absence of them. It seems, then, that only when the themes of tombs and patriotism were combined, did Freneau write conventional melancholy graveyard verse, as in "Stanzas Published at the Procession to the Tomb of the Patriots." The prison ship patriots "sunk, unpitied, in their bloom,—/ They scarcely found a shallow tomb/ To hide the naked bones." The melancholy exists, however, not for its own sake, not for the evocation of sentiment, but to urge Americans to greater deeds. The spirit of the dead shall last in order "to brighten and illume the mind,/ 'Till tyrants vanish from mankind/ And Tyranny is Done."

Howling wolves, a discolored moon, and the yew trees color the horror of "The House of Night," and ravens and bats are part and parcel of ruins and graveyards. But in his later poems Freneau rarely uses Gothic paraphernalia to induce melancholy or dread. In "Pestilence," he could have used such machinery and have written a poetic *Arthur Mervyn*. The poem, indeed, describes the same Gothic scene that Charles Brockden Brown used to produce horror in *Arthur Mervyn*, but Freneau disdains to evoke a shudder:

> Hot, dry winds forever blowing,
> Dead men to the grave-yards going:
> > Constant hearses,
> > Funeral verses;
> Oh! what plagues—there is no knowing!
>
> * * * *
>
> Nature's poisons here collected,
> Water, earth, and air infected—
> > O, what a pity,
> > Such a City,
> Was in such a place erected!

The rational once more dominates the emotional.

Although Freneau did not have moldering abbeys to inspire or initiate his mourning over times past, he did imitate the genre in the early "Upon an Ancient Farm-House" and in "Stanzas Occasioned by the Ruins of a Country Inn." The melancholy in the latter stems from both the ruins and the recollection of happier times. Thus, where once "full many a guest forgot his woes," now, "ravens here, with eye forlorn,/ And clustering bats henceforth will meet." The poet complains of Time, who might have spared the inn, but "alike

beneath whose potent sway/ A temple or a tavern falls." Unlike the
abbeys mourned for in England, however, this ruin may be rebuilt,
and then, "we again may quaff his wine,/ Again collect our jovial
crew." Thus the poet indicates his melancholy will be cured by a
very pragmatic solution.

Freneau makes no complaint in verse about being deprived of
Europe's ruins, and he rarely grieved over the passing of the past.
For him, mourning for times past was usually limited to the gentle
yearning for the past happiness of one man's life. "Ode on a Remote
Perspective View of Princeton College," while reminiscent of Gray's
"Ode on a Distant Prospect of Eton College," does not contain the
moralizing of Gray. Instead, Freneau portrays the joys and the
graver moments of his college days: "Still Fancy hears the midnight
prayer,/ Monitions mild—when, free from care,/ When smit with
awe, the attentive train/ Renounced the world, or owed it vain/
With penitential tear." The poem exudes a gentle melancholy, one
induced by the poet's fondness for his past happiness and by the
knowledge that such happiness can no longer be attained. The
melancholy is, however, implied, not directly expressed.

One of Freneau's last poems, although not one of his better ones,
rejects outright the fashion of mourning lost youth and past times.
"Answer to a Letter of Despondency" gives Freneau's prescription
for a melancholy friend:

> Your blood yet flows in youthful veins;
> Forsake the springs while yet you can,
> Trod mountain roads, and rough domains,
> And be, once more, the active man.
>
> The *spleen* is half your sad complaint:
> Be off-reject the nauseous draft,
> Which many a sinner, many a saint
> Have quaff'd, and cursed it while they quaff'd.

The poem ends, somewhat puzzlingly, with the cynical reminder
that the friend will be welcomed, especially if he carry "a generous
heart—and weighty Purse." This advice is rough: one should not be
melancholy, one should not dwell on the past but live actively in the
present, equipped, however, with full knowledge of the world's
ways. Despite its lack of success as a poem, "Answer to a Letter of
Despondency" does express Freneau's attitude of living life in the
present, with full recognition of the beauties and evils of the time.

VI *Poems on the Vanity of Existence*

Freneau's early poetry contains a number of verses that evoke melancholy by discussing death and the vanity of existence; usually, as in the popular English verse of the era, the subject is expressed by moralizing about the seasons. "The Vernal Ague" creates the emotion of melancholy in its first five stanzas, which are good examples of this type of pre-Romantic poetry. The poet is wandering in the midst of nature which has pleased him before but does so no longer:

> The winding stream, that glides along,
> The lark, that tunes her early song,
> The mountain's brow, the sloping vale,
> The murmuring of the western gale,
>
> Have lost their charms!—the blooms are gone!
> Trees put a darker aspect on.

In the last stanza, which unites the melancholy with thought of death, the poet asks Nature to "renew those colours, that must fade,/ When vernal suns forbear to roll,/ And endless winter chills the soul." While Nature will renew herself in spring, man's winter is final. In "The Season's Moralized," Freneau explicitly points out the analogy between the seasons and man's ages. The seasons form a cycle, but man's life does not: "Clad in the vestments of a tomb,/ Old age is only Winter's gloom—/ Winter, alas! shall spring restore,/ But youth returns to man no more." "The Seasons Moralized" contains a very conventional thought in a very conventional form.

Death, the seasons, and the vanity of existence are all united in another early poem, "Plato, the Philosopher, to His Friend Theon." Plato, who is seeking to inure Theon to the thought of death, warns him that "Autumnal seasons shall return,/ And spring shall bloom, but not for you." The death of man, however, fits into nature's plan: "The mountains waste, the shores decay,/ Once purling streams are dead and dry—/ 'Twas nature's work—'tis nature's play,/ And nature says that all must die." Having told his friend about the necessity of death and having indicated the harshness of mortal life, Plato advises Theon to "aspire where sweeter blossoms blow/ And fairer flowers bedeck the ground." Death is defined in the concluding stanza as "the freedom of the mind." Man fits into Nature's plan in facing bodily destruction; he is, however, an exception to that plan because part of him is indestructible.

As in "Plato," so also in his most famous life-is-in-vain poem, "The Vanity of Existence," Freneau presents the afterlife in favorable terms: "Death is to wake, to rise again/ To that true life you best esteem." Freneau follows the conventions of the genre in showing that life is short, harsh, and bitter: and he does so in order to present the glories of the life to come. Thus, in this poem, he states that life is a dream, that life after death is real and estimable. To support this statement, he uses an unconventional analogy to close the poem:

> So nightly on some shallow tide,
> Oft have I seen a splendid show;
> Reflected stars on either side,
> And glittering moons were seen below.
>
> But when the tide had ebbed away,
> The scene fantastic with it fled,
> A bank of mud around me lay,
> And sea-weed on the river's bed.

These stanzas of realistic description strengthen the originality of the poem but not Freneau's moral. If life is a dream, the dream can be correlated with the reflected "spendid show." When the dream (life, the tide) passes away, the result is mud (afterdeath). Although all analogies do not have to be perfect, the conclusion of the poem does not put the reader in an exalted frame of mind.

During Freneau's maturity, but not during his later years, he changed his attitude toward the afterdeath when he adopted the cyclical theory of Nature, as pointed out by Nelson Adkins in his *The Cosmic Enigma* (1949). Combining the atomic theory of the ancients with that of Sir Issac Newton, the theory posits a mechanistic universe that runs like clockwork. Freneau popularized this theory in a witty way in "On the Vicissitudes of Things," a poem originally written as verses for the newsboys to present to their customers on New Year's Day when they collected money for subscriptions. Again, the seasons are used as illustration: "They're hardly born before they die"; they are "like atoms round the rapid wheel." This passage of time, however, should not cause melancholy:

> How vain to sigh!—the wheel must on
> And straws are to the whirlpool drawn,
> With ships of gallant mien—
> What has been once, may time restore;

> What now exists, has been before—
> Years only change the scene.
>
> In endless circles all things move;
> Below, about, far off, above,
> This motion all attain—

Having expounded the theory, Freneau concludes the poem by pointing out that coins are circular too; therefore, cash goes "from you to us—from us it rolls/ To comfort other cloudy souls." We doubt whether another such scientific plea for customers' payment is extant.

For new healthy life to be created, there must be decay of the old—the decayed matter will not be lost; matter is preserved. This statement is true not only about plants but also about man. All does not end with the tomb, but is changed, altered, and returned to the life cycle—a logical extension of the cyclical theory. This thought is expressed in "On the Sleep of Plants," first published in 1790, which begins by pointing out that just as man sleeps at night, so do plants the botanists have discovered. But other resemblances exist between men and plants: "Like us, the slave of cold and heat,/ She too enjoys her little span":

> Thus, moulded from one common clay,
> A varied life adorns the plain;
> By Nature subject to decay,
> By Nature meant to bloom again!

In this middle period, Freneau does not make man the exception to the cyclical rule either by naming the grave as the end of life or by subscribing to the doctrine of a better life beyond the grave. Rather, man dies, decays, and from that decay new life, although different, is formed. Thus an earthly immortality is achieved: dust to life to dust, ashes to life to ashes.

To this period of Freneau's thinking belongs "The Wild Honey Suckle," one of his most often printed poems. First published in 1786, it concerns the life cycle of a common flower. This poem, well within the melancholy genre, consists of the poet's pensive musings on the flower's story. The first two stanzas picture the advantages of the flower's country retreat: "No roving foot shall crush thee here,/ No busy hand provoke a tear." Nature foreordained the honeysuckle's place:

> She bade thee shun the vulgar eye,
> And planted here the guardian shade,
> And sent soft waters murmuring by,
>   Thus quietly thy summer goes,
>   Thy days declining to repose.

The next stanza elaborates the analogy suggested by the mention of summer in the previous stanza; again Freneau unites the theme of the seasons with the thought that all must die:

> Smit with those charms, that must decay,
> I grieve to see your future doom;
> They died—nor were those flowers more gay,
> The flowers that did in Eden bloom;
>   Unpitying frosts, and Autumn's power
>   Shall leave no vestige of this flower.

Decay is the universal law, mourning is permissible, but there is yet more to say. Death and decay, as well as creation, are so common, so much a part of the universal law, that they lose their power to awe:

> From morning suns and evening dews
> At first thy little being came:
> If nothing once, you nothing lose,
> For when you die you are the same;
>   The space between, is but an hour,
>   The frail duration of a flower.

And yet, is there not something to regret that life is "but an hour"? The tone of the poem is, through all the stanzas, one of pensive melancholy. The tone is conventional, the themes are conventional, but all elements are so well combined that this poem rises above the conventional.

Although Freneau skillfully worked the usual themes to produce "The Wild Honey Suckle," we must remember that he was a satirist of conventions and a city poet as well as one of the country. Thus it is not too surprising to find him mocking the same themes he expressed so well in "The Wild Honey Suckle." The poem containing this mockery is "The Fading Rose," found in his 1809 edition. He begins the poem only half seriously:

> Adjacent to LUCINDA's *bed*,
> Or (rather than be thought ill bred)
> Adjacent to Lucinda's *room*
> A ROSE TREE, in the wane of bloom
> A serious course of lectures brings
> On the vanity of human things.

Lucinda grieves for the fading rose: "How pensively we saw her lean,/ And mourn the rose." But nothing can be done, "for Nature's law will be obeyed,/ Which raised such beauties from the plain,/ —To sink them in—to dust again!" Therefore, Lucinda composes an epitaph for her rose, and it has this as a last stanza:

> "Here, trampled, slighted, or forgot,
> And left, with common weeds, to rot;
> Gay flower!—once more, to make you live,
> Lucinda will some water give—
> With dregs of many a dish of tea
> The fair one will besprinkle thee:
> And thus, another birth secure,
> And prove the virtues of MANURE!"

All the themes of "The Wild Honey Suckle" are present in "The Fading Rose": the lonely flower fades away, the pensive mourner moralizes on the fading, assurance is given that all things die, the "dust to dust" theme is repeated—all are mocked by the very practical mention of manure. It is, as we have seen, not unusual for Freneau to mock the poetic conventions of the day, but the unusualness of his mocking his own well-expressed themes strikes us again and again.

In his earlier seasonal poetry, the correlations are fairly constant. Spring equals youth and joy; summer, the prime of man; autumn, maturity and ripened fruit; winter, old age, bleakness and desolation. In his later years, however, the images associated with autumn and winter change greatly. For instance, "October's Address," included in Freneau's 1815 edition, could be taken as a direct response to the earlier "The Vernal Ague." The setting is the same:

> "The flowers have dropt, their blooms are gone,
> The herbage is no longer green;
> The birds are to their haunts withdrawn,
> The leaves are scatter'd through the plain."

Instead of asserting that there is nothing left to charm one, as the poet did in the earlier poem, October asks the question rhetorically: " 'What have you left for comfort now,/ When all is dead, or seems to die/ That cheer'd the heart or charm'd the eye?' " October gives a positive answer to his own question: remaining is the pine whose leaves do not fall and which will give a cheery winter fire. Also remaining are eating, drinking, and female conversation. There is to be enjoyed " 'what reason will afford' ": " 'The cottage warm and cheerful heart/ Will cheat the stormy winter night,/ Will bid the glooms of care depart/ And to December give delight.' " Significantly enough, October is described as being "rather gay"; for this attitude is not the conventional one toward autumn or winter of Freneau's earlier poetry.

The same theme is repeated in a much lighter vein in "Stanzas on the Great Comet: To Ismenia." Freneau questions the nature of a comet that has just appeared, and he conjectures that there, "who knows but in yon flaming sphere/ The souls from parted bodies are." As the comet nears the sun, its spring and summer occur, then its autumn. As the comet becomes more remote from view, the next season arrives:

> Then is his winter, then his folks
> Sit snug at home and pass their jokes,
> No doubt, enjoy the evening fire,
> The glass, the parson, and the 'squire,
> See oceans rage, hear tempests blow,
> And scorn them all—as we do now.

Thus described, winter seems the best season of the year. Although no analogy is made between winter and old age, the poems are not lacking in philosophy; and we are tempted to enlarge Freneau's moral by asserting that happiness may be found in small ways, no matter the season or the age.

But this conclusion is not made explicit, even in Freneau's last known poem, titled "Winter." Written in rhyming couplets and in iambic pentameter, the poem shows Freneau taking more liberties with his meter than usual. The first stanza begins by pitying those who enjoy nature only in her better moods:

> The Sun hangs low!—So much the worse, we say,
> For *those* whose pleasure is a Summer's day;

> Few are the joys which stormy Nature yields
> From blasting winds and desolated fields.

In the second stanza the poet, as he did in "October's Address," again poses a rhetorical question: "But are no Joys to these cold months assign'd?" The answer is, of course, yes. There are joys that are not dependent on Nature's mood:

> Happy with wine we may indulge an hour;
> The noblest beverage of the mildest power.
> Happy, with Love, to solace every care,
> Happy with sense and wit an hour to share;
> These to the mind a thousand pleasures bring
> And give to winter's frosts the smiles of spring,
> Above all praise pre-eminence they claim
> Nor leave a sting behind—remorse and shame.

Above all things, "Winter" celebrated the neoclassic ideal of reason and moderation, the basis of the ideal life.

VII *Poems on the Pleasure of Country Life*

The ideal life of conventional poetry was one of retirement from the world, the life of philosophy, the life with nature, the life away from cities. Needless to say, this ideal was not a new one, but Freneau's age claimed it as its own. The picture of country contentment was derived from the neoclassic virtue of moderation; the pre-Romantics also accepted the vision of a quiet, retired way of living, among nature's beauties. The city was degraded; the country, exalted. Freneau, as he did with the other popular themes of the day, also celebrated the virtues of retirement. In "St. Catherine's," his emphasis is on the beauties of nature, and the remoteness of the spot from cities: "What pleasure strikes the mind,/ From Folly's train, thus wandering far,/ To leave the world behind." The scenery that the poet so admires is described, however, in conventional and somewhat incongruous Old World terms:

> The music of these savage groves
> In simple accents swells,
> And freely here, their sylvan loves
> The feather'd nation tells;
> The panting deer through mingled shades

> Of oaks forever green
> The vegetable world invades,
> That skirts the watery scene.

Such a natural scene temps the poet to remain, a hermit "in yonder fragrant vale."

While the beauties of nature are appreciated for themselves, they are appreciated even more for their simplicity in contrast to the complex follies and ambitions of men. While the ostensible object of "Neversink," one of Freneau's better poems, is the description of the hills, it is also a retirement to solitude poem. The hills become for the poet an object of worship:

> These heights, for solitude design'd,
> This rude, resounding shore—
> These vales impervious to the wind,
> Tall oaks, that to the tempest bend,
> Half Druid, I adore.

Henceforth, asserts the poet, he will stay by these hills:

> Let those who pant for wealth or fame
> Pursue the watery road;
> Soft sleep and ease, blest days and nights,
> And health, attend these favourite heights,
> Retirement's blest abode!

To get away from the folly of man, to find a secluded spot, to appreciate nature to be content—such is the poetic dream. The ideal of moderation can best be pursued in retirement.

But Freneau could appreciate nature in other places than the traditional "sequestered vale." The 1809 "Lines Written at Sea" departs from the conventional worship of natural beauties, although it retains Freneau's all too conventional meter:

> No pleasure on earth can afford such delights,
> As the heavenly view of these tropical nights:
> The glow of the stars, and the breeze of the sea,
> Are heaven—if heaven on ocean can be.

As if this last qualification had reminded him of the nonheavenly aspects, he then describes the sun, which had set and was enabled "to recline at his ease,/ And not, like ourselves, to be pestered with fleas." Having mentioned the harsh reality, the poet recalls himself; and he dreams of an island "where quarrels, and murder, and malice are not." But this island is not sought, as we might expect, to get away from the ways of men but for a more practical reason. He seeks an island "where a stranger might land, to recruit his worn crew,/ Replenish the casks, and the water renew." The rest of the poem is devoted to musings about nature's seemingly arbitrary placement of islands in the sea. The poem is not united, but it does illustrate Freneau's tendency to balance the ideal with the real.

Such balancing also occurs in "On a Rural Nymph," a poem that has been praised as being quite Romantic in nature, and so the first half of it is. Found in the 1815 edition, the poem portrays an encounter between an Englishman and a Madeira maid:

> Six miles, and more, with nimble foot
> She came from some sequestered spot,
> A handsome, swarthy, rustic maid
> With furze and fern, upon her head:
> The burthen hid a bonnet blue,
> The only hat, perhaps, she knew,
> No slippers on her feet were seen;
> Yet every step display'd a mein
> As if she might in courts appear,
> Though placed by wayward fortune here.

The unexpected encounter of loveliness in an out-of-the-way spot is an often treated Romantic theme. Here, the man tries to persuade the beauty Dulcina to come to London with him and promises her all sorts of finery. She, however, refuses; she is contented with her lot, her place in nature. Her description of her life, in its simplicity, also would appeal to the Romantic:

> She said, "before the sun was up
> I finish'd with my chocolate cup:
> A hank of yarn I fairly spun,
> And, when the hank of yarn was done,
> To have a fire, and cook our mess
> I travell'd yonder wilderness;
> I climb'd a mountain very tall,
> Unwearied, and without a fall,
> And gather'd up this little pack
> Which now you see me carrying back."

Had the poem ended here, it would have indeed presented a Wordsworthian picture. But it does not. Instead, Freneau evidently feels compelled to protest against the conditions which he has so romantically described. He speculates whether the girl throve by climbing hills, and states that, as in her case, where kings exist, "the common herd are poor and mean." If, however, Dulcina had lived where liberty was, she would have had her man, plus a horse and cow:

> She would have had, to save her feet,
> A pair of shoes and suit complete.
> A decent dress, and not of rags,
> A state above the rank of hags;
> A language if not over fine,
> At least above the beggar's whine.

With the inclusion of this last stanza, the picture that seemed so romantic before now seems much less so. We forget the charming picture and conceive the reality, the harshness of the maid's life. The final effect of the poem is not that left by Wordsworth's "The Solitary Reaper."

Freneau was too honest to picture the "nymphs and swains" of rural America as being as happy as he implies in the first part of "On a Rural Nymph." Although he talks generally and conventionally about the pleasure of country life, he just as often produces a realistic picture of that life. In "The Forest Beau," he pictures a rural suitor who is courting his maid: he shaves his beard, soles his shoes, cuts a cane, and sets off, "in thought a beau, a savage to the eye," bearing his gift of tobacco for the girl. He woos, the gift pleases, he is accepted. He builds a hut for her in the woods, and the only idealistic touch is "there sees the summer pass and winter come,/ Nor envies Britain's king his loftier home." In other poems dealing with the condition of the small farmer, however, the conclusion is not so pat. A late poem, "Elijah, the New England Emigrant," is a four-part picture of the plight of a young New England couple who farm a small parcel of land. While the poem is chiefly intended to satirize New England ways (there is much mention of onions, and Blue Laws, Providence, and restlessness—the same objects of satire as Irving's New England descriptions in *Knickerbocker's History*), we find more realistic descriptions within the poem, as when Elijah describes the condition of the soil:

> "This field, this soil, so old and worn,
> Has seen two hundred crops of corn:
> Here *onions* throve in seasons past,
> But *onions* will not always last;
> Here, *barley* grew some years ago,
> But barley will not always grow.
> At least, it grows so poor and lean
> I am ashamed it should be seen;
> I did my best to make manure
> But blights and blasts have made us poor."

Susannah's contributions to the household add little; of her truck garden, only the pumpkins do well. She works at the spinning wheel, "which made Susannah's fingers red,/ Chafed by the furrows of the thread,/ And little got for all her labor." Faced by this poverty, the couple plan to migrate to the West, where Elijah anticipates a far better fortune. When they mention their intention to Susannah's father from whom they rent their land, Hezekiah tells them to be content where they are:

> "And in your brains this proverb toss,
> *A rolling stone collects no moss.*
> A farm on *Alabama's* streams
> Might do in JOEL BARLOW'S dreams . . .
> Such rhyming dealers in romance
> See Nature only in a trance.—"

The hard-headed farmer's advice displeases the young couple, and they resolve to leave Hezekiah and the five years of rent they owe him behind.

Had they read Freneau's "Log-Town Tavern" first, they might have been content to stay where they were. In this poem, Freneau locates the tavern in the pine barrens of North Carolina and gives a picture of the backwoods life—a picture far from being a poetic dream. The town of logs boasts a log inn, whose landlord, "gouged in either eye,/ Here drains his bottle to the dregs,/ Or borrows Susan's pipe, while she/ Prepares the bacon and the eggs." The entertainment of the evening is furnished by "a rambling hag," who "screeched out a song." The walls are covered with graffitti: "with scraps of songs and smutty words/ Each lodger here adorns the walls:/ The wanton muse no pencil gives,/ A coal her mean idea scrawls." The poet dines on moldy corn pone, surrounded by sleeping pigs. Needless to say, he warns others away: "O may they never venture near,/ Such fleas and filthiness abound."

But such dreariness was not limited to the backwoods. In "The Bay Islet," Freneau pictures the life of those on a small island near New York City. There the poet found "no blooming goddesses" but "yellow hags, ordained to prove/ The death, and antidote of love." The house is "a crazy, tottering pile"; and the pastures are inhabited by six hogs. While the picture is grim, the poet sees that it could be improved: he suggests that someone with money should "to this neglected spot repair:/ What Nature sketched, let art complete,/ And own the loveliest Country Seat." But, without money, without art, rural life is not enviable.

Freneau, who often plays with the ideal of "pure" nature, juxtaposes the ideal with reality. In "The Passaick Garden," he envisions the place as "Paradise complete," the Garden of Eden without the serpent:

> For here we find a sweet repose,
> And here a heavenly river flows:
> Dame Nature here is calm and kind,
> Nor has one frown that we can find:
> Another system all would seem,
> And so we think, or so we dream.

The vision so delights the poet of the poem that he swears that nothing should tempt him from the garden. But he wakes from his poetic vision to the reality: "Here runs at large a yelping cur,/ And there the Jockey—whip and spur—." A tavern is near by, with its various noises and battling customers: "Their tongues are loud, the men are bold,/ And mastiffs growl and women scold,/ And drunkards reel, and children squall." All in all, the poet concludes, if this is Paradise, "I seize my staff, and pray for grace/ To find it in—some other place." Despite the poet's complaint, this is a good-humored poem; we cannot help feeling the speaker really does not mind having his vision shattered. The closing picture of reality, in fact, is the poet's device for mocking the idealistic garden picture.

If any of Freneau's poetry views nature with a touch of mysticism, this quality is found in his poetry of the sea. In his land poems, nature is discussed in terms either of the seasons or of man—even his descriptions of secluded spots are populated with hermits, nymphs, and swains—who are either Indian or white. In his more realistic poems, untamed Nature is that which has not been adequately tamed by man; and Freneau expresses scorn for men who have not applied their arts to her. But nature in his sea poems becomes something man can do nothing about. What may be Freneau's best sea poem, "A Midnight Storm in the Gulph Stream," shows his unostentatious treatment of a sensational theme. His earlier poem, "The Hurricane," contrasts the tumult of the sea and the dire forebodings of sailors finding their coral beds with the cheerful shore. "A Midnight Storm. . . ," about essentially the same subject, proceeds less dramatically, although we are made fully aware of the danger involved. There is lightning and thunder, and "strange fires the watery wave illume,/ That inlet to eternity!" Yards and masts creak, the sails may not hold, the seamen grip the lines for safety: "What yet avails, what yet remains/ But anxious hearts, and toil severe." Freneau describes the pumps being manned, another deluge endured, then nothing but acceptance: "How feeble are the strongest hands,/ How weak all human efforts prove!—/ He who obeys, and who commands/ Must await a mandate from above." The last stanza, which relates the outcome of the storm, is very restrained, for Freneau lets his description alone convey the emotion:

> 'Tis done!—we view in western skies
> The clouds dispersed, and stars appear;
> Before the blast the vapour flies;
> The waves subside their awful swell,
> The *starboard* watch hails, All is well!
> And from the land again we steer.

In one of his letters, Freneau commented that the life of the sea made man a true philosopher: if his sea poems reveal any special philosophy, it is that elemental pleasures are the ones to be savored.

Appreciation of simple, elemental things includes gratitude for human kindness. In two late companion poems, Freneau presents pictures of a lovely country seat and the nearby wigwam of an Indian. Of the two dwellings, the Indian's is favored—not because of its placement in wild, untamed nature but because of the inhabitants' hospitality. The title of the first, "Verses Written on Leaving a Great House of Much Ceremony, but Little Sincerity, or

Hospitality," adequately describes the content; the subheading, "CAUTION" thoroughly reinforces the title. Consideration is lacking at the house "Beaurepaire," no matter what effort the guest makes to be acceptable:

> You comb your hair, you brush your coat
> Almost to thread-bare to the neat,
> Yet, in its *knap* a single spot
> Will be observed by all you meet:
> And you will be no more caress'd,
> Be censured as a *clown* at best.

The poem's spokesman, disgusted, resolves to seek a warmer welcome with Indian Sam. "The Arrival at Indian Sam's (Or, Wee-Quali's) Wigwam" is the companion piece—one of Freneau's more interesting poems. The character of the spokesman, delineated in "On Leaving a Great House," is sustained, as is that character's bitterness at "Beaurepaire." Indian Sam is pictured as a man and not as a noble savage. The woods are described realistically and not designated as "verdure," or some such general term. Despite the built-in interest belonging to a visit to an Indian camp, Freneau does not let the purpose of the poem be forgotten: the interest in Indian Sam lies not in his being an Indian, but in his being so generous despite his poverty.

Almost the first half of the poem is description of the way to the hut. The visitor had been told of an old Indian path, and Freneau draws a realistic picture of what happens to anyone who is unsure of his way in the woods:

> The Indian path was blind indeed,
> O'er run with shrubs and hemlock weed,
> My stockings torn, and scratched my face
> I soon was in a shocking case;
> But thanked my stars, as matters were,
> I was not bound for *Beaurepaire*.

Finally, the visitor approaches the light of the camp. A dog barks, his master calls to know who is there, and the traveler answers with a bitter description of the place he has come from. The Indian's response is colloquial:

> You come, you say from *Beaurepaire!*—
> Good man, what devil took you there?—
> I sell them *game,* and let me tell you
> They never pay me half the value.
> They are a lofty minded sett,
> Of high designs—but deep in debt—

Then Sam welcomes the traveler to share his squirrels and venison, adding that *"We-quallis* is my Indian name,/ By *that* I am by most address'd/ But *Sam's* intended for a Jest." The traveler's horse is fed, as it was not at Beaurepaire; and the stranger enters a hut in which he finds little furniture; for the squaw and three papooses sleep on mats of straw: "But yet enough for such as these/ Whom very little serves to please;/ It was not rich, and something rare,/ But quite unfit for *Beaurepaire.*" The traveler stays three days. When he leaves, the Indian promises to show him to the turnpike, "too near, alas! to this abode," and warns him to avoid "Beaurepaire" next time. Unfortunately for Freneau's intention, we are more interested in his picture of the Indian living among white men and selling his game to them (a realistic picture rare this early in American literature) than in the poet's moral about the virtues of kindness and hospitality.

VIII   *The Indian Poems*

Some critics have called Freneau's Indian poems his best work—they have been considered to be both realistic and Romantic. With one or two exceptions, however, the Indian poems most often reprinted are not original in content. The American Indian figured in drama, poetry, and prose during most of the eighteenth century; the poetry corners of the newspapers often included poems on dying Indians, warriors' laments, and Indian prophecies. In a collection of Indian poems of the eighteenth century, it would be very difficult to separate those poems written by the English, who had never seen any but captive Indians brought to London, and the Americans, who might have seen the Indian in his natural habitat.

Convention ruled the contents of these poems; to the Indian, the virtues of the Romans were ascribed; to his way of life, the characteristics of the Greek and Roman visions of the past Golden Age were given. While H. N. Fairchild makes the distinction between the satirist who "uses the savage as a convenient weapon" and the romanticist who "sees him as an embodiment of a creed,"[14] there seems to me to be a third classification: the poet of melancholy who uses the Indian to evoke pathetic emotion. Freneau's poems fit these classifications: he used the Indian to satirize white men's folly (as with Indian Sam); he used him to evoke melancholy; and he used the Indian to bolster his creed—not the Romantic creed but that of the Enlightenment in which all nature is ruled by universal laws. Freneau's thesis is that the Indian's life-style most follows such laws.

"The Dying Indian," an early poem, has as its motive the evocation of melancholy; its theme is the nature of Death. Tomo-Chequi faces death stoically, although the afterlife is not pictured as a happier land but as a gloomy one: "What solitary streams,/ In dull and dreary dreams,/ All melancholy, must I rove along!" Life after death, in Tomo-Chequi's mind, suffers by contrast to the here and now. In the "groves of the dead," he envisions no hunting, no life-giving vegetation: "But sickly orchards there/ Do fruits as sickly bear,/ And apples a consumptive visage shew,/ And withered hangs the hurtle-berry blue." Only in the last stanza of the poem is the gloom and dejection relieved as Tomo-Chequi speculates that "Nature at last these ruins may repair,/ When fate's long dream is o'er, and she forgets to weep/ Some real world once more may be assigned,/ Some new born mansion for the immortal mind!" This thought, which comforts the Indian, is but a repetition of Freneau's cyclical theory which stresses the value of life over that of the afterlife. "The Dying Indian" is unusual because the speaker has an unconventional attitude toward death; in addition, this Indian is more of a philosopher than most.

"The Prophecy of King Tammany" contains a more conventional treatment of the Indian attitude toward death. The chief on his funeral pyre, "smiled amid the fervours of the fire/ To think his troubles were so near their end." His soul "sought the world unknown, and dark oblivion's shade." This poem, like the rest of Freneau's Indian poems, is not, however, a good example of the popular type; for the poet uses Tammany for his own political purposes. Although Tammany describes, in conventional manner, the ills done to his tribe by the white man, his prophecy concentrates on the ills to befall the colonists in their turn: "Hostile squadrons for your blood shall come." In two other Indian poems, Freneau uses the Indian as a device for satire; for in the first poem,

"The Indian Convert," he describes the efforts to convert the Indians to the Christian faith. Finally, the one Indian who agrees to attend church questions the minister on heaven. The preacher tries to enlighten him: "The place I'm describing is most like our meeting,/ Good people, all singing, with preaching and prayer;/ They live upon these without eating or drinking." At this, the Indian says farewell: "On victuals, so airy, I faintish should feel,/ I cannot consent to be lodged in a place/ Where there's nothing to eat and but little to steal." Although this Indian is logical (objecting to this concept of heaven on the same grounds that Mark Twain was to later), he is not—with the mention of stealing—a Noble Savage.

More noble is the Indian of a second poem, "The Indian Student," which describes the consequence of sending him to college in the hopes that his education would speed conversion. The Indian departs for the college, "where learned men talk heathen Greek,/ And Hebrew lore is gabbled o'er,/ To please the Muses,—twice a week." But the student soon casts Virgil aside in favor of the more familiar woods, and he regrets that he had exchanged them for his new knowledge:

> "A little could my wants supply—
> Can wealth and honour give me more;
> Or, will the sylvan god deny
> The humble treat he gave before?
>
> "Let seraphs gain the bright abode,
> And heaven's sublimest mansions see—
> I only bow to Nature's God—
> The land of shades will do for me."

"The Indian Student: Or, Force of Nature" is partly a satire of the folly of the college authorities and partly a celebration of life lived in harmony with nature.

One of Freneau's later poems demonstrates his concern with the effects of the white man's culture on the Indian. He pleads for restraint in "On the Civilization of the Western Aboriginal Country":

> THOU, who shalt rove the trackless western wastes
> Tribes to reform, or have new *breeds* embraced,
> Be but sincere!—the native of the wild

> If wrong, is only Nature's ruder child;
> The arts you teach, perhaps not ALL amiss,
> Are arts destructive of domestic bliss.

The poem is more than this warning—it is one of Freneau's most complex poems in that he tries in it to reconcile emotion and philosophy. He feels for the Indian, but he perceives their life-style must be changed. Indeed, the first philosophical principle Freneau asserts in the poem is that Nature operates by cycles: "Some stars, worn out, have ceased to shine or burn,/ And some, relumed, to their old posts return." With one hand, Nature creates; with the other, she destroys; and only "matter, deathless matter, still remains."

This principle he then applies to the Indian. The Indian, converted to a ploughman, passes from the style of living where he thought only for the day. Mourning the change, he cannot view this new life as the white man does:

> Of different mind, he sees not with your sight,
> Perfect, perhaps, as viewed by Nature's light:
> By Nature's dictates all his views are bent,
> No more *imperfect* than his AUTHOR meant.

Freneau is obviously faced with a problem. If the rational eighteenth-century man, convinced that he has penetrated to the laws of nature, sees the settling of the West as necessary to progress, then the poetic, simple life-style of the Indian, so long celebrated as ideal, must be altered.

Freneau's solution of this dilemma is to conclude that the white man must, indeed, change the Indian; but, in so doing, he must act morally. To reach this conclusion, he posits another basic principle: a true religion must have been common to men in all ages and in all places. As he expresses it, "all moral virtue, joined in one vast frame,/ In forms though varying, still endures the same." Those who settle the West, driven by the wrong motives, leave "where simple Nature reign'd,/ A thousand *Vices* for one *Virtue* gained." Freneau, however, relents toward those who go with the right motives— motives which are unselfish and in accord with reason:

> Go, and convince the natives of the west
> That *christian* morals are the first and best;

> And yet *the same* that beam'd thro' every age,
> Adorn the *ancient,* or the modern page;
> That without which, no social compacts bind,
> Nor *honor* stamps her image on mankind.

In short, he says, "go, teach what Reason dictates should be taught."
But the settler also should be prepared to learn from the Indians
their great truth: "Take all, through all, through nation, tribe, or
clan,/ The child of Nature is the *better* man."

This poem is a difficult one because Freneau is trying to reconcile
so many different ideas. He shifts from moods of melancholy to
disgust to confidence. And the final statement, "the child of Nature
is the *better* man," can only be understood in context. All things
flourish and die in their turn, and so the Indian must. But there are,
despite this fact, certain eternal truths which the Indian embodies.
The white man, in displacing the Indian, must also live in accord
with these truths. All men, Indian or white, whatever their place or
civilization, who live more in accordance with Nature's rules as
revealed by reason, are the better men.

IX *Philosophical Poetry*

Freneau's opinion of the nature of man's moral state varied according to the various periods of his life and, we suspect, according
to his opinion of contemporary events. Sometimes he views man as
good; sometimes, as evil. Sometimes he places the golden age of
man in the future with the implication that he can improve himself;
sometimes that golden age is located in the past—man has fallen
away from its perfection. In "On a Nocturnal View of the Planet
Jupiter," Freneau's fancy leads him to populate that planet and to
speculate about man's future existence there. But the genius of the
planet speaks against the project:

> "If man were once admitted here
> His madness would distract my sphere;
> He would perplex, intrigue, ensnare,
> And every shape of mischief wear.
> He would torment, intrigue, derange,
> And half my lovely system change,
> And make my globe (to wars unknown)
> The horrid image of his own."

To Freneau the rational satirist, man is innately foolish. He could, however, change his attitudes when it suited him; and it suited him in "On the Abuse of Human Power, As Exercised over Opinion," to present an entirely different picture of man. Possibly occasioned by the Alien and Sedition laws, the protest against any attempt to coerce man's judgment is based on the philosophy that man, unrestrained, is "no artist to some evil end,/ But good and great, benign and just,/ As God and nature made them first." This affirmation, however, is rare in Freneau's works.

In most poems, he sought to reassure himself and his countrymen that the future held a brighter world. He had hailed the European revolutions for more freedom as proof that men were finally on their way to that world; the failure of those revolutions meant revision of this philosophy. His period of greatest doubt occurred in 1798 during Adams' presidency when it appeared certain that the United States would join with Britain in a war against France. Poems from this period contain the message that man has stepped back from his progress; but, hopefully, he will resume it. Freneau appears most doubtful of his philosophy of progress in "On False Systems of Government, and the Generally Debased Condition of Mankind." He asks, "does there exist, or will there come/ An age with wisdom to assume,/ The Rights by heaven designed." The age, if it is to come, must belong to republics, for monarchies are degenerate. To reach that age, man must be reformed, and laws must be enacted to tame man's passions and greed. Then, "men will rise from what they are," a progress made surer because men still own some of their previous goodness, "which full, which fair, which perfect shone/ When love and peace, in concord sown,/ Ruled, and inspired each breast." Thus, although man has "missed the state by Nature planned," the possibility exists that he may yet achieve it.

The poem does not end on this note of subdued hopefulness but on one of pessimism and doubt:

> What are the ends of Nature's laws;
> What folly prompts, what madness draws
> Mankind in chains, too strong:—
> Nature, to us, confused appears,
> On little things she wastes her cares,
> The great seem sometimes wrong.

This pessimism and doubt contrast with Freneau's many other assertions of the justness and reasonableness of Nature's laws and with the confidence of "The New Age: Or, Truth Triumphant" in which he proclaims, "I saw the blest benignant hour/ When the worst plague of human race,/ Dread superstition, lost her power." The loss of this power is but a prelude to the next step when "sovereign truth prevails at last/ To triumph o'er the errors past." I cynically suspect that this poem was written at a time when Freneau was satisfied with human events. Apparently he never hesitated to publish a poem because its thought conflicted with that of his other poems.

Freneau was a cynic himself when someone else was predicting the coming of the millenium. In "Ode X: To Santone Samuel," Freneau mocks the prophet's vision that "the lion and the lamb will stray,/ And, social, walk the woodland way." If the lion ever betrays his teeth and claws, "he will be changed to something new/ And have some other part to do." So with man: "Ere discord can from man depart/ He must assume a different heart." Freneau does indeed acknowledge the possibility that "our race may rise,/ By reason's aid to stretch their wings"; but his doing so will be far off: "you and I will not be here/ To see the lion shed his teeth/ Or kings forget the trade of death." At this point in his life (1797), Freneau seems resigned to unchanging human nature.

The events surrounding the War of 1812 inspired Freneau to write many reflections in which he attempts to adjust to his disappointment at the seeming reversal of man's progress—the best of which is "The Brook of the Valley." He uses the brook as an analogy to men and nations; the tone is resigned; the verse form and style is reminiscent of William Blake's *Songs of Innocence*. After a prefatory stanza, in which Freneau sets the scene (war has come again, but the brook still runs), the poet addresses the brook directly:

> All pacific as you seem:
> Such a gay elysian stream;—
> Were you always thus at rest
> How the valley would be blest.
>
> But, if always thus at rest;
> This would not be for the best:
> In one summer you would die
> And leave the valley parch'd and dry.

Still addressing the brook, Freneau describes the cycle of the waters: to the ocean, evaporated by the sun, converted to rain, to the

brook again. After the rain, "lately, angry, how you ran!/ All at war—
and much like man." Now at peace, the brook will, in time, rage out
of its banks again. So, the brook is an emblem of man: "Muddy now,
and limpid next,/ Now with icy shackles vext—/ What a likeness
here we find!/ What a picture of mankind!" In this poem, the poet
takes care to impress us with the cycles of the brook—and, by
extension, with the cyclical nature of man's history. Acceptance of
the adage "history repeats itself" carries the implication of lack of
progress; for, if man goes in circles, he is not advancing directly
toward a goal. Freneau's fondness for cyclical theories here betrays
his desire to see the progress of man.

Although many of Freneau's cycles were derived from the
neoclassics' reading of Lucretius, another source early influenced
him in favor of cycles. In 1786, he wrote a verse review of Emanuel
Swedenborg, "On a Book Called Unitarian Theology." The ideas
that Freneau celebrates in this poem are the depiction of "One
Power of Love, that fills unbounded space," and the reasoning about
the afterlife where the parted souls meet in the ideal world:

> All there is Mind!—That Intellectual Flame,
> From whose vast stores all human genius came,
> In which all Nature forms on Reason's plan—
> Flows to this abject world, and beams on Man!

Like brook waters which are continuously recycled, the intellectual
energy of the world is pictured by Freneau as emmanating from,
and as returning to, one great reservoir, the "Power of Love." But
he had moved away from the Plotinus-like "One Power of Love" by
his 1809 edition to a conception of the ruling power as a being whose
main quality was orderliness. Nonetheless, "Reflections on the
Constitution, or Frame of Nature," still emphasizes the oneness of
the power, although it is now remote from man—nature is its
immediate effect:

> THOU, nature's self art nature's God
> Through all expansion spread abroad,
> Existing in the eternal scheme,
> Vast, undivided, and supreme.
>
> *   *   *   *
>
> Its powers, still active, never rest,
> From motions, by THAT GOD impressed,
> Who life through all creation spread,
> Nor left the meanest atom dead.

The primary being set the world in order and put it in motion. All was perfect; there was no need for heavenly intervention.

From this general neoclassic reading of the universe, Freneau moved to a more individual, although similar reading. Four poems in the 1815 edition are essentially versification of ideas expressed in Thomas Paine's *Age of Reason*. The conclusion of "The Uniformity and Perfection of Nature" ("All, nature made, in reason's sight/ Is order all, and *all is right*") brings Alexander Pope's "One truth is clear, Whatever is, is right" immediately to mind; but the argument of the poem is a rephrasing of Paine's objection to miracles. Nature, Paine and Freneau say, works according to fixed laws; and exceptions cannot be made:

> Could she descend from that great plan
> To work unusual things for man
> To suit the insect of an hour—
> This would betray a want of power.

Any miracle, or breaking of the laws, would imply that the original design was imperfect.

Paine also argued that the truest scriptures are those truths universally accepted by man in all times and in all places. In "Belief and Unbelief," Freneau, in rephrasing this concept, keeps something of Paine's tone:

> They who extort belief from man
> Should, in the out-set of their plan,
> Exhibit, like the mid-day sun
> An evidence denied by none.

The greatest scripture, Paine felt, was Nature herself; for she was common to all men in all times; and Freneau agrees in "On the Religion of Nature." Nature, a moralist, teaches man his duty: "Born with ourselves, her early sway/ Inclines the tender mind to take/ The path of right, fair virtue's way." This gift is given to all, and the power is a joyful one: "This deals not curses to mankind,/ Or dooms them to perpetual grief." By reading the book of nature, man finds God; and the poet describes Him as constantly present—as no longer the remote God of his earlier poems: "In seas, on earth, this God is seen;/ All that exist upon him lean;/ He lives in all, and never stray'd/ A moment from the works he made." With this poem, "On the Universality and other Attributes of the God of Nature," Freneau has returned to the concept of a loving God: "He all things into *being* loved;/ O'er all he made he still presides,/ For them in life, or death provides."

It is possible that Freneau again revised his theology late in life. At least, in his last poems, he seems more tolerant, and less assured that he knows how God works. One poem, first printed in 1816, phrases the doctrines he earlier argued against—those of the traditional theology of the Calvinists. The poem, occasioned by a small boy who narrowly escaped being struck by a rattlesnake, is entitled "Stanzas Written for a Lad." The poem is too little known; it is very simple, but somehow satisfactory:

> Eternal praise to thee, my God,
> Who guards me when the danger's nigh,
> Preventing all my steps abroad
> From lighting on the serpent sly.
>
> How near was I to death's cold shade,
> When the other step had been my last,
> But *thou* art still my constant aid,
> Both for the present and the past.
>
> *   *   *   *
> Or, had thy vision so decreed,
> That his cursed head should bruise my heel;
> And, for my sins, that I should bleed,
> Thy judgment had been righteous still.
>
> The subtle poison through each vein,
> Had then thy God-like image foiled,
> And, through excess of rage and pain,
> Faint nature had in death recoiled.—
>
> Since GOD of me hath mindful been,
> To guard me from this treacherous foe,
> My endless praises he shall win
> And all the world his mercies know.

This poem, with its traditional doctrine of an intervening God, is not Freneau's theology as we know it; but the lines convey sincerity. The transition from the actual to the biblical serpent is well done; the implicit acceptance of God's ways and the tone remind us of the poems of Edward Taylor or Anne Bradstreet, and especially of the latter because of the hiatus in thought between the next-to-last and the last stanza. But, despite the biblical allusions and the doctrine, this poem remains essentially a child's prayer, for the last stanza is like a prayer before bedtime.

In another late poem, "Philosophical Fortitude," Freneau expresses some of his earlier sentiments but also admits that we cannot be sure of Nature's plan. It, also, is a poem of resignation. The first stanza presents the idea that, while the vicious fear death, the virtuous do not. The second stanza, much longer, contains a collection of ideas. He repeats the concept of the perfection of Nature's laws: "Ills from ourselves, and not from Nature flow,/ And true Religion never leads to woe." Having stated this, he then limits inquiry:

> 'Tis ours to improve this life, not ours to know
> From whence this *meteor* comes, or where shall go,
> This *mind*, this *spark*, that animates our frame,
> Directs, impels, and still remains the same.

The wise, relying on the kind judgment and mercy of heaven, depend on death; they wait to "quit the vain scene, where few have found or know/ The first grand purpose—*why we live below.*" Thus man should be virtuous and trust to the grand design of the universe. This poem is one of the few philosophical ones by Freneau in which reason is slighted and in which faith becomes the motive for leading a virtuous life.

Freneau also recognized that the life we live is often not ideal; that often even the virtuous are punished. "On the Evils of Human Life" accounts for those evils rather simply by stating that they are not evils in nature's larger plan:

> The ills that God, or nature, deal,
> The ills we hourly see, or feel,
> The sense of wretchedness and wo
> To man may be sincerely so;
>> And yet these springs of tears and sighs
>> Be heaven's best blessings in disguise.

But Freneau also recognized that even reasonable men who most practiced virtue could not avoid misfortune. In "On Happiness, as Proceeding from the Practice of Virtue," he sought to justify this anomaly. If the virtuous person encounters misfortune, he is more able to overcome it; if, however, his whole life is unfortunate, "another life has heaven design'd/ Where she her due rewards will find." He even has an answer for those who do not believe in the heavenly afterlife: "to be conscious we have done/ The worthy part, though frown'd upon,/ Can every seeming ill destroy." Thus Freneau, while never dealing directly with the problem of the existence of evil in a perfect world, nevertheless comes close to Candide's final answer: one must cultivate his own garden.

Freneau's abstract poems on the great questions of the universe are, in a different way, as imitative as his melancholy poems. He versified the great questions of the age and did so in abstract language, for he uses very few concrete details or examples and only an occasional analogy. These are essentially scholarly poems that illustrate his reading more than they illustrate his poetic ability. Occasionally, however, in dealing with good and ill fortune, Freneau casts his scholarship aside and returns to his colloquial style. "Ode to Good Fortune" begins traditionally enough with an address to Good Fortune: "Thou great first wish! well understood,/ But not for all design'd;/ Bestow'd alike on bad and good,/ Since, fortune you are blind." He soon abandons the classic style and gets down to particulars. He asks that knaves not steal his money, "for we, as well as they, must live,/ And debts as surely pay." He asks that Fortune not allow "one voracious maw/ Thy dainty things be fed" while others go to bed without supper. He asks the means to pay the boardinghouse. He does not ask for gourmet meals—only that he be saved from an empty stomach. But his plea extends further:

> Help us for hungry folk to feel
> When hungry folk we see;
> May I with sharpers learn to deal
> As sharpers deal with me.

In essence, this plea is not for good fortune; it is a request that he be allowed to go the middle way, not soaring to any heights, but not sinking to the depths either:

> This day be bread and cheese my lot,
> With glass of apple wine;
> To morrow, if roast pigs, or not,
> Is no concern of mine.
>
> O thou, whose frowns are no disgrace,
> But yet whose smiles I prize,
> Do, let me have some humble place,
> But not to grandeur rise—

The poem is one of acceptance of life as it is but one, however, that evinces full awareness of its lack of ideality. There is hunger, and there are knaves and "sharpers" in the world—the evil must be accepted, just as the good must be. The only plea is: "Give us this day our daily bread."

Looking over the body of Freneau's nonoccasional poems, we find inconsistency in thought and a great variety in style, tone, and subject matter. He was an imitative poet—when it suited him; more often than not, he satirized the genre in which some of his most famous poems are included. A prolific poet, he seems to have versified almost every thought, every speculation that entered his mind, every idea he considered worthwhile from his reading. Often didactic, sometimes humorously mocking didacticism, his work is more neoclassic than not, although we can find examples to place in almost every classification of poetry that was written during his era. His better poems are those which are not so imitative—those in which he allows himself to show his humor, his wit, his roughness. He was scolded by critics during his lifetime for his low language and common subjects, but the poems exhibiting these traits are now better appreciated. His meter is all too often too regular; and, all too often, the poems lack unity and a single focus. What makes these poems worthwhile is their complexity of thought, occasionally their simply expressed emotion, or their wittily expressed perception of folly.

Summation

ANY judgment of Freneau's worth as a littérateur is difficult. He set in train no literary school; if his work influenced any later artists, they did not credit it. What influence his work had was chiefly exerted on his contemporaries and was felt not because of the artistry of the works, but because of their "gadfly" qualities. Today, we can criticize most of his works as imperfect, as somehow defective. We can see where, in this essay or that poem, he excelled himself and achieved art. But other writers have achieved art more consistently than Freneau did; in the history of literature, there are many better essayists and better poets.

But few in the history of American literature have contributed a total body of works so rich and so wide—so much a reflection of the life lived in his age. Freneau shows us the life lived by rich and poor; by stable-boy, slave, and president; by backwoodsman and city dweller. He records the great events of the day as well as the personal tragedies and triumphs. He writes in all the styles of the day, and he also mocks them when they violate his sense of decorum. He reflects the changing attitudes toward religion, and the various theories of the universe. He shows the discoveries of the new science, and he mocks it when it seems to exceed its bounds. Freneau's study is man in all his variety and complexity, and the totality of Freneau's works reflects back to us man's variety. This reflection is Freneau's value for us.

The following poem, one not reprinted to my knowledge since Freneau's 1809 edition, typifies to me the essence of this poet. Written in his even meter and rhyme (even in this being typical), the poem captures the spirit of a man who fully recognizes the reality, the evil and folly of this world; who is hampered by it; but who nevertheless keeps the ideal in front of him. He does not passively accept the evil; he "growls" at it and progresses toward his goal.

173

ESPERANZA'S MARCH:

Being Stanzas Addressed to a Person who Complained *"He was Always Unfortunate."*

He stood with his front to the north,
His hat was encumbered with snow;
His purse was a purse of no worth,
His walk was the valley of woe.

His brow was the image of care,
He sighed when he saw it his lot—
He thought he had more than his share,
But said, he regarded it not.

Wherever he stept or he trode
Some trouble or obstacle lay;
No level he saw on his road
For mountains obstructed his way:

Above him were harpies and hawks,
And vultures, with horrible shrieks;—
Some gave him unmerciful strokes,
Some struck at his eyes with their beaks.

Around him were tygers and bears,
All hoping to feast on his beef;
Beneath him deceptions and snares
Occasioned some flurries of grief.

The hurricane blew from the pole
Direct to the point he was bound—
It tried all the stuff in his soul,
And whistled incessantly round.

If, 'chance he ascended a hill
The ruffians were seen on his track,
And, if they designed not to kill,
They pulled the poor traveller back.

And when he attained to some bluff
And downward began to progress,
Each gave him a thump or a shove
Though no one could merit it less.—

Enraged at the ills he essayed
He raised up his staff, with a frown;
"And why all this malice (he said)
And why are you pushing me down?

Not one of you all have I harmed,
I quietly travel my path;
Yet vultures and devils are armed
To teaze with their rancour and wrath:

My object I swear to attain
The house that is built on the hill—
You strive to prevent me—in vain—
For reach it I certainly will."

So forward he went, with a growl,
That frightened the insolent crew;
They fled from his sight with a howl
And left him his road to pursue.

He rose above malice and spite,
His courage and conduct displayed—
'Till the palace he gained on the height,
Which all his disasters repaid.

Freneau regarded himself as a gentleman, a poet, a ship's captain and a farmer: during his lifetime he was regarded as a party hack, only secondarily as a poet. Late in his life, after time had mellowed the Jeffersonian party feuds, Freneau was honored as "The Poet of the Revolution," and welcomed to submit his verse for celebrations of that event. His prose, if not forgotten, was "kindly" not mentioned. Much the same attitude toward Freneau prevails today. Most anthologies of American authors include Freneau's most famous poems: "The Wild Honey Suckle," possibly the "Vanity of Existence," selections from "The House of Night," a humorous poem, an Indian poem, a late philosophical poem (often "On the Uniformity and Perfection of Nature". Except for "Eutaw Springs," little of his Revolutionary verse is published. None of his prose is published in these anthologies—that he was one of the better essayists of the day is forgotten. Today, Freneau is known for a few poems, for being Jefferson's newspaper editor, and for being "The Poet of the American Revolution." Time has simplified his complexity.

Notes and References

Chapter One

1. William Nelson, ed., *Documents Relating to the Colonial History of the State of New Jersey, Archives of the State of New Jersey*, 1st ser. vol. 26, pp. 383–84.
2. Lewis Leary, ed., *The Last Poems of Philip Freneau* (New Brunswick, 1945), p. 100.
3. H. H. Clark, "The Literary Influences of Philip Freneau," *Studies in Philology* 22 (January, 1925), 3.
4. *The Last Poems*, p. 102.
5. William T. Hutchinson and William M. E. Rachal, eds., *The Papers of James Madison* (Chicago, 1962) I, 4.
6. Matthew L. Davis, *Memoirs of Aaron Burr* (New York, 1852), I, 37.
7. W. Jay Mills, ed., [William Paterson], *Glimpses of Colonial Society and the Life at Princeton College* (Philadelphia, 1903), p. 35.
8. Jacob N. Beam, *The American Whig Society of Princeton University* (Princeton, 1933), p. 52.
9. Hutchinson, ed., *Papers of James Madison* I, 65.
10. Claude Milton Newlin, *The Life and Writings of Hugh Henry Brackenridge* (Princeton, 1932), p. 15.
11. Lewis Leary, ed., Hugh Henry Brackenridge and Philip Freneau, "Father Bombo's Pilgrimage," *Pennsylvania Magazine* 66 (October, 1942), 467.
12. Nelson, ed., *Documents*, p. 203.
13. *Ibid.*, p. 584.
14. Fred Lewis Pattee, ed., *Poems of Philip Freneau* (Princeton, 1902), p. xxiv.
15. Mary S. Austin, *Philip Freneau: The Poet of the Revolution* (Detroit, 1968), pp. 80–81.
16. Hutchinson, ed., *Papers of James Madison*, I, 103.
17. Arthur M. Schlesinger, *Prelude to Independence: The Newspaper War on Great Britain* (New York, 1958), pp. 183–210.
18. Hutchinson, ed., *Papers of James Madison*, I, 126.
19. *Ibid.*, p. 135.

20. Ibid., p. 73.

21. Lewis Leary, *That Rascal Freneau* (New Brunswick, 1941), p. 42.

22. John Butt, ed., *The Poems of Alexander Pope (New Haven* 1966), pp. 196–97.

23. *The American Village*, intro. Harry Lyman Koopman, facsimile reproduction (Providence, 1906), p. 6.

24. Leary, *That Rascal Freneau, p.* 55.

Chapter Two

1. "Account of the Island of Santa Cruz," *United States Magazine* 1 (February, 1779), 82.

2. Ibid., p. 83.

3. Ibid. 1 (March, 1779), 124.

4. Philip M. Marsh, ed., *The Prose of Philip Freneau* (New Brunswick, 1955), p. 479.

5. James Curtis Ballagh, ed., *The Letters of Richard Henry Lee* (New York, 1914), II, 230.

6. Clark, pp. 9–10.

7. "The Loyalists," *United States Magazine* 1 (July, 1779), 315–16.

8. *Some Account of the Capture of the Ship Aurora (*New York, 1899), p. 49.

9. Gardner W. Allen, *A Naval History of the American Revolution* (New York, 1962), II, 627.

10. *The Prose of Philip Freneau,* p. 92.

Chapter Three

1. George Gibbs, *Memoirs of the Administration of Washington and John Adams Edited from the Papers of Oliver Wolcott* (New York, 1846), I, 107.

2. Harold C. Syrett, ed., *The Papers of Alexander Hamilton* (New York, 1969), XII, 196.

3. Gibbs, p. 79.

4. Marsh, ed., *The Prose of Philip Freneau,* p. 263. All references to contributions to the *Daily Advertiser* are taken from this volume.

5. "To the Public," *National Gazette,* October 31, 1791, p. 1. Further quotations of contributions to this paper are taken directly from the *National Gazette.*

6. Matthew L. Davis, *Memoirs of Aaron Burr* (New York, 1852), I, 306.

7. "To the Public," *Jersey Chronicle,* May 2, 1795, p. 1. All further quotations of contributions to this paper are taken directly from the *Jersey Chronicle.*

8. "To the Public," *The Time Piece, and Literary Companion*, March 13, 1797, p. 1. Quotations from this paper come directly from *The Time Piece.*

9. Marsh, ed. *The Prose of Philip Freneau*, p. 42. Quotations from "The Pilgrim" are taken from this source.

10. *The Miscellaneous Works of Mr. Philip Freneau* (Philadelphia, 1788), p. 285. Quotations from *Miscellaneous Works* are taken from this edition.

11. "Tomo Cheeki, the Creek Indian in Philadelphia," *The Time Piece, and Literary Companion*, March 15, 1797, p. 8. Quotations of the "Tomo Cheeki" essays are from this source.

12. "On the Culture of Pumpkins. By Hezekiah Salem, late of New England," *The Time Piece, and Literary Companion*, October 23, 1797, p. 1. All quotations from "Hezekiah Salem" are from this source.

13. *Letters on Various Interesting and Important Subjects*, intro. Harry Hayden Clark (New York, 1943), p. 15. Further quotations from the *Letters* follow this edition.

Chapter Four

1. Austin, p. 204.

2. Frank Smith, "Philip Freneau and The *Time-Piece and Literary Companion*," *American Literature* 4 (November, 1932), 287.

3. Pattee, p. lxxx.

4. Leary, p. 325.

5. Austin, pp. 196–97.

6. Ibid, p. 197.

7. Ibid., p. 205.

8. Charles F. Heartman, ed., *Unpublished Freneauana* (New York, 1918), p. 12.

9. Heartman, p. 16.

10. Ibid., p. 15.

11. Pattee, p. lxxxv.

12. Nelson F. Adkins, *Philip Freneau and the Cosmic Enigma* (New York, 1949), p. 68.

13. Clark, p. 9.

14. Hoxie N. Fairchild, *The Noble Savage: A Study in Romantic Naturalism* (New York, 1961), p. 52.

Selected Bibliography

PRIMARY SOURCES

The best bibliography of Freneau's published works is in Lewis Leary's *That Rascal Freneau* (New Brunswick: Rutgers University Press, 1941), pp. 418–80.
1. Major works published during Freneau's lifetime.
The American Village, a Poem. New York: printed by S. Inslee and A. Car, 1772.
The British Prison-Ship: A Poem. Philadelphia: F. Bailey, 1781.
A Collection of Poems, on American Affairs. 2 vols. New York: David Longworth, 1815.
A Journey from Philadelphia to New-York. Philadelphia: Francis Bailey, 1787.
Letters on Various interesting and important Subjects. Philadelphia: printed by D. Hogan, 1799.
The Miscellaneous Works of Mr. Philip Freneau. Philadelphia: Francis Bailey, 1788.
The Monmouth Almanac for the Year M, DCC, XCV. Middletown-Point: P. Freneau, 1794.
A Poem, on the Rising Glory of America. Philadelphia: printed by Joseph Crukshank for R. Aitken, 1772.
The Poems of Philip Freneau. Philadelphia: Francis Bailey, 1786.
Poems written and published during the American Revolutionary War. 2 vols. Philadelphia: Lydia R. Bailey, 1809.
Poems Written between the Years 1768 & 1794. Monmouth: Philip Freneau, 1795.

2. Newspapers carrying significant contributions.
Aurora. Philadelphia, 1799–1800.
City Gazette. Charleston, 1788–1790, 1800–1801.
Daily Advertiser. New York, 1789–1791.
Freeman's Journal. Philadelphia, 1781–1788.
Jersey Chronicle. Monmouth, 1795–1796.
National Gazette. Philadelphia, 1791–1793.
New-York Weekly Museum. 1816.

Time Piece. New York, 1797–1798.
True American. Trenton, 1821–1824.
United States Magazine. Philadelphia, 1779.

3. Later editions of Freneau's works.

The American Village: A Poem by Philip Freneau. Introduction by Harry Lyman Koopman. Providence: Club for Colonial Reprints of Providence, Rhode Island, 1906.

"Father Bombo's Pilgrimage." Edited by Lewis Leary. *Pennsylvania Magazine* 66 (October, 1942), 459–78.

The Last Poems of Philip Freneau. Edited by Lewis Leary. New Brunswick: Rutgers University Press, 1945.

Letters on Various Interesting and Important Subjects. Introduction by Harry Hayden Clark. New York: Scholars' Facsimiles & Reprints, 1943.

Poems of Freneau. Edited by Harry Hayden Clark. New York: Hafner Publishing Company, 1960.

Poems of Philip Freneau. Edited by Fred Lewis Pattee. 3 vols. Princeton: The University Library, 1902.

The Prose of Philip Freneau. Edited by Philip M. Marsh. New Brunswick: The Scarecrow Press, 1955.

Some Account of the Capture of the Ship Aurora. Introduction by Jay Milles. New York: M. F. Mansfield & A. Wessels, 1899.

Unpublished Freneauana. Edited by Charles F. Heartman. New York: printed for the author, 1918.

SECONDARY SOURCES

1. Works on Freneau

ADKINS, NELSON F. *Philip Freneau and the Cosmic Enigma*. New York: New York University Press, 1949. Good, thorough study of Freneau's theological and philosophical speculations.

AUSTIN, MARY S. *Philip Freneau*. New York: A. Wessels Company, 1901. Biography contains many letters of Freneau; interesting (although not trustworthy) for its reliance on Freneau family legend.

AXELRAD, JACOB. *Philip Freneau: Champion of Democracy*. Austin: University of Texas Press, 1967. Biography; concentrates on Freneau as patriot.

BATTEN, CHARLES L., JR. "A Newly Discovered Poem by Philip Freneau on the Death of General Moreau." *American Literature* 44 (November, 1972), [457]–59. Discovery of new poem in Freneau's handwriting.

CLARK, HARRY HAYDEN. "The Literary Influences of Philip Freneau," *Studies in Philology* 22 (January, 1925), 1–33. Valuable for giving books available to Freneau and the authors who influenced him.

COLLINS, JOHN F. "Two Last Poems of Freneau." *Early American Litera-*

ture 7 (Fall, 1972), 111–19. Gives a final stanza to "Winter," ascribes "The Vale of Obscurity" to Freneau.

GUMMERE, RICHARD M. "Apollo on Locust Street." *Pennsylvania Magazine* 56 (1932), 68–92. Criticizes Freneau for overuse of his classical knowledge.

LEARY, LEWIS. "Philip Freneau." I *Major Writers of Early American Literature*, ed. Everett Emerson, pp. 245–71. Madison: University of Wisconsin Press, 1972. Emphasis on Freneau's poetic characterizations and on a few good poems.

————. *That Rascal Freneau.* New Brunswick: Rutgers University Press, 1941. The standard biography of Freneau. If there is a bias, it is in the emphasis on Freneau's Romanticism.

MARSH, PHILIP M. "Freneau and Jefferson," *American Literature* 8 (May, 1936), 181–89. Chronicles the history of Jefferson's and Freneau's connection through the *National Gazette*.

————. *Freneau's Published Prose: A Bibliography.* Metuchen, N.J.: The Scarecrow Press, 1970. Lists both certain and probable items.

————. *Philip Freneau: Poet and Journalist.* Minneapolis: Dillon Press, 1967. A biographical and critical study; contains research since Leary's *That Rascal Freneau.*

————. *The Works of Philip Freneau: A Critical Study.* Metuchen, N.J.: The Scarecrow Press, 1968. Balanced treatment of both prose and poetry.

PATTEE, FRED LEWIS. "Life of Philip Freneau." *Poems of Philip Freneau.* Princeton: The University Library, 1902. I, xii–cxii. Good, basic introduction to Freneau.

SMITH, FRANK. "Philip Freneau and the Time-Piece and Literary Companion," *American Literature* 4 (November, 1932), 270–87. Gives the history (including letters by Freneau) of his attempt to establish this New York newspaper.

2. Works offering historical background of Freneau's era.

ALLEN, GARDNER W. *A Naval History of the American Revolution.* 2 vols. New York: Russell & Russell, Inc., 1962. Thorough study of the naval war.

BATE, WALTER JACKSON. *From Classic to Romantic.* Cambridge: Harvard University Press, 1946. "Classic" study of the shift in poetic theory and mood taking place during Freneau's time.

BEAM, JACOB N. *The American Whig Society of Princeton University.* Princeton: published by the Society, 1933. History of the literary club Freneau joined in college.

BRIDENBAUGH, CARL. *Cities in Revolt.* New York: Alfred A. Knopf, 1955. Cites economic and social conditions before the war.

CUNNINGHAM, NOBLE E., JR. *The Jeffersonian Republicans.* Chapel Hill:

University of North Carolina Press, 1957. Traces national party disputes during the years of Freneau's editorships.

DAVIDSON, PHILIP. *Propaganda and the American Revolution: 1763–1783.* Chapel Hill: University of North Carolina Press, 1941. Charts the decrease of Whig and the rise of loyalist propaganda.

DAVIS, MATTHEW L. *Memoirs of Aaron Burr.* 2 vols. New York: Harper & Brothers, 1836. Good chronical of the activities (at Princeton and as an Anti-Federalist) of this contemporary of Freneau's.

FAIRCHILD, HOXIE N. *The Noble Savage: A Study in Romantic Naturalism.* New York: Russell and Russell, 1961. Thorough study of the treatment of the Indian in this period of English literature.

FRANCIS, JOHN W. *Old New York: Or, Reminiscences of the Past Sixty Years.* New York: Charles Roe, 1858. Memories of the postwar years by Freneau's friend.

GIBBS, GEORGE. *Memoirs of the Administrations of Washington and John Adams: Edited from the Papers of Oliver Wolcott.* New York: William Van Norden, 1846. History of the first presidencies told from a definite Federalist point of view.

GRISWOLD, RUFUS WILMOT. *The Republican Court: American Society in the Days of Washington.* New York: D. Appleton and Company, 1867. Early history which accepts unreservedly the greatness of the Federalists and the moral weakness of the Jeffersonians.

HAMILTON, ALEXANDER. *The Papers of Alexander Hamilton.* Edited by Harold C. Syrett. Vols. XI, XII, XIV. New York: Columbia University Press, 1969. Letters concerning Freneau and the *National Gazette.*

JEFFERSON, THOMAS. *The Writings of Thomas Jefferson.* Edited by Albert Ellery Bergh. Vols. VIII, XIX. Washington, D.C.: The Thomas Jefferson Memorial Association, 1907. Letters concerning Freneau.

KERR, WILFRED BRENTON. *Bermuda and the American Revolution: 1760–1783.* Princeton: Princeton University Press, 1936. Gives the state of Bermuda and the West Indies at the time Freneau explored them.

LINK, EUGENE PERRY. *Democratic-Republican Societies, 1790–1800.* New York: Columbia University Press, 1942. History of the "radical" clubs formed by men who were also proponents of the French Revolution.

MADISON, JAMES. *The Papers of James Madison.* Edited by William T. Hutchinson and William M. E. Rachal. Vols. I–III. Chicago: University of Chicago Press, 1962. Early letters from Freneau and concerning Freneau.

———. *The Writings of James Madison.* Edited by Gaillard Hunt. Vol. VI. New York: G.P. Putnam's Sons, 1906. Letters concerning Freneau's *National Gazette.*

MAIN, JACKSON TURNER. *The Antifederalists: Critics of the Constitution 1781–1788.* Chapel Hill: University of North Carolina Press, 1961. Covers the party conflicts of the years Freneau was newspaper editor.

MARSH, PHILIP M., ed. *Monroe's Defense of Jefferson and Freneau Against Hamilton*. Oxford, Ohio: Philip M. Marsh, 1948. Background and reprinting of Monroe's defense against the charges of Jefferson's hiring Freneau to be party editor.

MONROE, JAMES. *The Writings of James Monroe*. Edited by Stanislaus Murray Hamilton. Vol. I. New York: G. P. Putnam's Sons, 1898. Letters concerning the *National Gazette*.

NEWLIN, CLAUDE MILTON. *The Life and Writings of Hugh Henry Brackenridge*. Princeton: Princeton University Press, 1932. Standard biography of Freneau's contemporary and sometime collaborator.

SCHACHNER, NATHAN. *The Founding Fathers*. New York: A. S. Barnes & Co., 1970. General history of the events and men of the Revolutionary era.

SCHLESINGER, ARTHUR M. *Prelude to Independence: The Newspaper War on Great Britain*. New York: Alfred A. Knopf, 1958. Thorough study of newspaper controversies before the war.

SICKELS, ELEANOR M. *The Gloomy Egoist: Moods and Themes of Melancholy from Gray to Keats*. New York: Columbia University Press, 1932. Describes fashionable poetic manners and mannerisms of Freneau's age.

TINKCOM, HARRY MARLIN. *The Republicans and Federalists in Pennsylvania*. Harrisburg: Pennsylvania Historical and Museum Commission, 1950. Gives details of local party disputes (some involving Freneau).

Index

(The works of Freneau are listed under his name)